OTHER BOOKS BY PARKER J. PALMER

Parker J. Palmer

Author of *The Courage to Teach*

LET YOUR LIFE
SPEAK

LISTENING
FOR THE VOICE
OF VOCATION

Published by Jossey-Bass
A Wiley Imprint
989 Market Street, San Francisco, CA 94103-1741   www.josseybass.com

Jossey-Bass books and products are available through most bookstores. To contact Jossey-Bass directly call our Customer Care Department within the U.S. at 800-956-7739, outside the U.S. at 317-572-3986, or fax 317-572-4002.

Jossey-Bass also publishes its books in a variety of electronic formats. Some content that appears in print may not be available in electronic books.

Credits are on page 117.

Library of Congress Cataloging-in-Publication Data

Palmer, Parker J.
Let your life speak: listening for the voice of vocation /
Parker J. Palmer.
    p. cm.
  Includes bibliographical references.
  ISBN 0-7879-4735-0 (acid-free)
  1. Vocation—Christianity. I. Title.
  BV4740 .P35 2000
  248.4—dc21   99-6467

Printed in the United States of America
FIRST EDITION
HB Printing   F10017715_022120

ᗉ CONTENTS

For Heather Marie Palmer
my granddaughter

May you always treasure true self . . .

ᑖ GRATITUDES

With the exception of Chapter I, every chapter in this book originally appeared as an essay in some other publication during the past decade. I have rewritten all the essays, most of them substantially. My aim has been to create a real book—not just a collection of articles about vocation, but a coherent exploration of a subject that engages many of us for the better part of our lives.

I mention the provenance of these pieces partly because I believe in truth in labeling and partly because the people who invited me to write the original essays, with all the trust that implies, are valued partners in my own vocation.

Chapter II, "Now I Become Myself," was originally given as the G. D. Davidson Lecture at Warren Wilson College in Swannanoa, North Carolina, and published by the college as a pamphlet.[1] The unusual charge that accompanies the lectureship helped frame this book: reflect on your life story through the concept of vocation—"including lessons learned from disappointments and failures as well as successes"—and do so in a way that might speak to younger as well as older adults. I am grateful to my friend Doug Orr, president of the college, for extending the invitation; to Don and Ann Davidson for endowing a lectureship that invites this sort of reflection; and to the entire Warren Wilson community for receiving my words with such deep hospitality.

Chapter III, "When Way Closes," was originally written for *Weavings*, a quarterly journal of spirituality, at the request of its editor, John Mogabgab.[2] John, my good friend for many years, is one of the best companions a person could have along the way, and *Weavings*—the journal he has raised up from its infancy—is widely regarded as one of the finest periodicals of its kind.

Chapter IV, "All the Way Down," was originally written for a special issue of *Weavings* on the theme of the "wounded healer" in memory of Henri Nouwen.[3] Henri was a treasured friend and mentor to both John Mogabgab and me, and this chapter is testimony to the transcendent power of friendship. It explores my experience with depression, a subject I could not have dealt with so openly except for the support of friends still living and the spirit of a friend now gone.

Chapter V, "Leading from Within," was originally given as a speech for the Indiana Office of Campus Ministries, which published it as a pamphlet.[4] I am grateful to my friend Max Case, executive director, for his invitation and encouragement. Indeed, I am grateful to the many campus ministers, priests, and rabbis across the country who helped me take first steps toward my calling thirty years ago, at a time when few in the academy were willing to entertain spiritual questions, at least not in public—a situation that is, blessedly, different today.

Chapter VI, "There Is a Season," was written at the request of Rob Lehman, president of the Fetzer Institute and my good friend and co-conspirator in vocation, to help dedicate Fetzer's retreat center, Seasons. The Institute published this essay as a pamphlet that is placed in the bedrooms at Seasons to invite guests into reflection.[5] I think of that pamphlet as Fetzer's equivalent of the Hilton's "pillow mints"—and I think of Rob Lehman as a pioneer in empowering so many of us to explore the complex connections between inner and outer life.

Special thanks go to Sarah Polster, my editor at Jossey-Bass. She was the first to see that the question of vocation was at the heart of many of the essays I have written in recent years and to believe in their potential to become a real book. Her skillful editing has helped bring these essays together in a fabric more tightly woven than I could have achieved on my own.

My thanks also go to the other members of the Jossey-Bass staff who have been such superb partners in publishing: Carol Brown, Joanne Clapp Fullagar, Paula Goldstein, Danielle Neary, Johanna Vondeling, and Jennifer Whitney.

Much of the personal journey I trace in this book was made in the company of, and with the support of, members of my family, past and present. I did not include them in my narrative simply because their stories belong to them alone;

the only tale I know how to tell, or have a right to tell, is my own. But I thought of my family often and with deep gratitude as I was writing about the parts of the journey we shared.

To Sally Palmer, Brent Palmer, Todd Palmer, and Carrie Palmer: thank you for all the love you have given me along the way.

To Heather Palmer: thank you for the new love and laughter you have brought into my life—though I'd be grateful if you would stop reminding me to eat my vegetables!

To Sharon Palmer: thank you for your gifted editing that is vital to my vocation as a writer and for the love that sustains me as I learn how to let my life speak.

Madison, Wisconsin   Parker J. Palmer
July 1999

CHAPTER I

Listening to Life

> Some time when the river is ice ask me
> mistakes I have made. Ask me whether
> what I have done is my life. Others
> have come in their slow way into
> my thought, and some have tried to help
> or to hurt: ask me what difference
> their strongest love or hate has made.
>
> I will listen to what you say.
> You and I can turn and look
> at the silent river and wait. We know
> the current is there, hidden; and there
> are comings and goings from miles away
> that hold the stillness exactly before us.
> What the river says, that is what I say.
> —William Stafford, "ASK ME"[1]

"Ask me whether what I have done is my life." For some, those words will be nonsense, nothing more than a poet's loose way with language and logic. Of course what I have done is my life! To what am I supposed to compare it?

But for others, and I am one, the poet's words will be precise, piercing, and disquieting. They remind me of moments when it is clear—if I have eyes to see—that the life I am living is not the same as the life that wants to live in me. In those moments I sometimes catch a glimpse of my true life, a life hidden like the river beneath the ice. And in the spirit of the poet, I wonder: What am I meant to do? Who am I meant to be?

I was in my early thirties when I began, literally, to wake up to questions about my vocation. By all appearances, things were going well, but the soul does not put much stock in appearances. Seeking a path more purposeful than accumulating wealth, holding power, winning at competition, or securing a career, I had started to understand that it is indeed possible to live a life other than one's own. Fearful that I was doing just that—but uncertain about the deeper, truer life I sensed hidden inside me, uncertain whether it was real or trustworthy or within reach—I would snap awake in the middle of the night and stare for long hours at the ceiling.

Then I ran across the old Quaker saying, "Let your life speak." I found those words encouraging, and I thought I understood what they meant: "Let the highest truths and values guide you. Live up to those demanding standards in everything you do." Because I had heroes at the time who seemed to be doing exactly that, this exhortation had incarnate meaning for me—it meant living a life like that of Martin Luther King Jr. or Rosa Parks or Mahatma Gandhi or Dorothy Day, a life of high purpose.

So I lined up the loftiest ideals I could find and set out to achieve them. The results were rarely admirable, often laughable, and sometimes grotesque. But always they were unreal, a distortion of my true self—as must be the case when one lives from the outside in, not the inside out. I had simply found a "noble" way to live a life that was not my own, a life spent imitating heroes instead of listening to my heart.

Today, some thirty years later, "Let your life speak" means something else to me, a meaning faithful both to the ambiguity of those words and to the complexity of my own experience: "Before you tell your life what you intend to do with it, listen for what it intends to do with you. Before you tell your life what truths and values you have decided to live up to, let your life tell you what truths you embody, what values you represent."

My youthful understanding of "Let your life speak" led me to conjure up the highest values I could imagine and then try to conform my life to them whether they were mine or not. If that sounds like what we are *supposed* to do with values, it is because that is what we are too often taught. There is a simplistic brand of moralism among us that wants to reduce the ethical life to making a list, checking it twice—against the index in some best-selling book of virtues, perhaps—and then trying very hard to be not naughty but nice.

There may be moments in life when we are so unformed that we need to use values like an exoskeleton to keep us from collapsing. But something is very wrong if such moments recur often in adulthood. Trying to live someone else's life, or to live by an abstract norm, will invariably fail—and may even do great damage.

Vocation, the way I was seeking it, becomes an act of will, a grim determination that one's life will go this way or that whether it wants to or not. If the self is sin-ridden and will bow to truth and goodness only under duress, that approach to vocation makes sense. But if the self seeks not pathology but wholeness, as I believe it does, then the willful pursuit of vocation is an act of violence toward ourselves—violence in the name of a vision that, however lofty, is forced on the self from without rather than grown from within. True self, when violated, will always resist us, sometimes at great cost, holding our lives in check until we honor its truth.

Vocation does not come from willfulness. It comes from listening. I must listen to my life and try to understand what it is truly about—quite apart from what I would like it to be about—or my life will never represent anything real in the world, no matter how earnest my intentions.

That insight is hidden in the word *vocation* itself, which is rooted in the Latin for "voice." Vocation does not mean a goal that I pursue. It means a calling that I hear. Before I can tell my life what I want to do with it, I must listen to my life telling me who I am. I must listen for the truths and values at the heart of my own identity, not the standards by which I *must* live—but the standards by which I cannot help but live if I am living my own life.

Behind this understanding of vocation is a truth that the ego does not want to hear because it threatens the ego's turf: everyone has a life that is different from the "I" of daily consciousness, a life that is trying to live through the "I" who is its vessel. This is what the poet knows and what every wisdom tradition teaches: there is a great gulf between the way my ego wants to identify me, with its protective masks and self-serving fictions, and my true self.

It takes time and hard experience to sense the difference between the two—to sense that running beneath the surface of the experience I call my life, there is a deeper and truer life waiting to be acknowledged. That fact alone makes "listen to your life" difficult counsel to follow. The difficulty is compounded by the fact that from our first days in school, we are taught to listen to everything and everyone but ourselves, to take all our clues about living from the people and powers around us.

I sometimes lead retreats, and from time to time participants show me the notes they are taking as the retreat unfolds. The pattern is nearly universal: people take copious notes on what the retreat leader says, and they sometimes take notes on the words of certain wise people in the group, but rarely, if ever, do they take notes on what they themselves say. We listen for guidance everywhere except from within.

I urge retreatants to turn their note-taking around, because the words we speak often contain counsel we are trying to give ourselves. We have a strange conceit in our culture that simply because we have said something, we understand what it means! But often we do not—especially when we speak from a deeper place than intellect or ego, speak the kind of words that arise when the inner teacher feels safe enough to tell its truth. At those moments, we need to listen to what our lives are saying *and* take notes on it, lest we forget our own truth or deny that we ever heard it.

Verbalizing is not the only way our lives speak, of course. They speak through our actions and reactions, our intuitions and instincts, our feelings and bodily states of being, perhaps more profoundly than through our words. We are like plants, full of tropisms that draw us toward certain experiences and repel us from others. If we can learn to read our own responses to our own experience—a text we are writing unconsciously every day we spend on earth—we will receive the guidance we need to live more authentic lives.

But if I am to let my life speak things I want to hear, things I would gladly tell others, I must also let it speak things I do not want to hear and would never tell anyone else! My life is not only about my strengths and virtues; it is also about my liabilities and my limits, my trespasses and my shadow. An inevitable though often ignored dimension of the quest for "wholeness" is that we must embrace what we dislike or find shameful about ourselves as well as what we are confident and proud of. That is why the poet says, "ask me mistakes I have made."

In the chapters to come, I speak often of my own mistakes—of wrong turns I have taken, of misreadings of my own reality—for hidden in these moments are important clues to my own vocation. I do not feel despondent about my mistakes, any more than the poet does, though I grieve the pain they have sometimes caused others. Our lives are "experiments with truth" (to borrow the subtitle of Gandhi's autobiography), and in an experiment negative results are at least as important as successes.[2] I have no idea how I would have learned the truth about myself and my calling without the mistakes I have made, though by that measure I should have written a much longer book!

How we are to listen to our lives is a question worth exploring. In our culture, we tend to gather information in ways that do not work very well when the source is the human soul: the soul is not responsive to subpoenas or cross-examinations. At best it will stand in the dock only long enough to plead the Fifth Amendment. At worst it will jump bail and never be heard from again. The soul speaks its truth only under quiet, inviting, and trustworthy conditions.

The soul is like a wild animal—tough, resilient, savvy, self-sufficient, and yet exceedingly shy. If we want to see a wild animal, the last thing we should do is to go crashing through the woods, shouting for the creature to come out. But if we are willing to walk quietly into the woods and sit silently for an hour or two at the base of a tree, the creature we are waiting for may well emerge, and out of the corner of an eye we will catch a glimpse of the precious wildness we seek.

That is why the poem at the head of this chapter ends in silence—and why I find it a bit embarrassing that as this chapter ends, I am drawing the reader not toward silence but toward speech, page after page of speech! I hope that my speech is faithful to what I have heard, in the silence, from my soul. And I hope that the reader who sits with this book can hear the silence that always surrounds us in the writing and reading of words. It is a silence that forever invites us to fathom the meaning of our lives—and forever reminds us of depths of meaning that words will never touch.

CHAPTER II

Now I Become Myself

A VISION OF VOCATION

With twenty-one words, carefully chosen and artfully woven, May Sarton evokes the quest for vocation—at least, my quest for vocation—with candor and precision:

> Now I become myself.
> It's taken time, many years and places.
> I have been dissolved and shaken,
> Worn other people's faces. . . .[1]

What a long time it can take to become the person one has always been! How often in the process we mask ourselves in faces that are not our own. How much dissolving and shaking of ego we must endure before we discover our deep identity—the true self within every human being that is the seed of authentic vocation.

I first learned about vocation growing up in the church. I value much about the religious tradition in which I was raised: its humility about its own convictions, its respect for the world's diversity, its concern for justice. But the idea of "vocation" I picked up in those circles created distortion until I grew strong enough to discard it. I mean the idea that vocation, or calling, comes from a voice external to ourselves, a voice of moral demand that asks us to become someone we are not yet—someone different, someone better, someone just beyond our reach.

That concept of vocation is rooted in a deep distrust of selfhood, in the belief that the sinful self will always be "selfish" unless corrected by external forces of virtue. It is a notion that made me feel inadequate to the task of living my own life, creating guilt about the distance between who I was and who I was supposed to be, leaving me exhausted as I labored to close the gap.

Today I understand vocation quite differently—not as a goal to be achieved but as a gift to be received. Discovering vocation does not mean scrambling toward some prize just beyond my reach but accepting the treasure of true self I already possess. Vocation does not come from a voice "out there" calling me to become something I am not. It comes from a voice "in here" calling me to be the person I was born to be, to fulfill the original selfhood given me at birth by God.

It is a strange gift, this birthright gift of self. Accepting it turns out to be even more demanding than attempting to become someone else! I have sometimes responded to that demand by ignoring the gift, or hiding it, or fleeing from it, or squandering it—and I think I am not alone. There is a Hasidic tale that reveals, with amazing brevity, both the universal tendency to want to be someone else and the ultimate importance of becoming one's self: Rabbi Zusya, when he was an old man, said, "In the coming world, they will not ask me: 'Why were you not Moses?' They will ask me: 'Why were you not Zusya?'"[2]

If you doubt that we all arrive in this world with gifts and as a gift, pay attention to an infant or a very young child. A few years ago, my daughter and her newborn baby came to live with me for a while. Watching my granddaughter from her earliest days on earth, I was able, in my early fifties, to see something that had eluded me as a twenty-something parent: my granddaughter arrived in the world as *this* kind of person rather than *that*, or *that*, or *that*.

She did not show up as raw material to be shaped into whatever image the world might want her to take. She arrived with her own gifted form, with the shape of her own sacred soul. Biblical faith calls it the image of God in which we are all created. Thomas Merton calls it true self. Quakers call it the inner light, or "that of God" in every person. The humanist tradition calls it identity and integrity. No matter what you call it, it is a pearl of great price.

In those early days of my granddaughter's life, I began observing the inclinations and proclivities that were planted in her at birth. I noticed, and I still notice, what she likes and dislikes, what she is drawn toward and repelled by, how she moves, what she does, what she says.

I am gathering my observations in a letter. When my granddaughter reaches her late teens or early twenties, I will make sure that my letter finds its way to her, with a preface something like this: "Here is a sketch of who you were from your earliest days in this world. It is not a definitive picture—only you can draw that. But it was sketched by a person who loves you very much. Perhaps these notes will help you do sooner something your grandfather did only later: remember who you were when you first arrived and reclaim the gift of true self."

We arrive in this world with birthright gifts—then we spend the first half of our lives abandoning them or letting others disabuse us of them. As young people, we are surrounded by expectations that may have little to do with who we really are, expectations held by people who are not trying to discern our selfhood but to fit us into slots. In families, schools, workplaces, and religious communities, we are trained away from true self toward images of acceptability; under social pressures like racism and sexism our original shape is deformed beyond recognition; and we ourselves, driven by fear, too often betray true self to gain the approval of others.

We are disabused of original giftedness in the first half of our lives. Then—if we are awake, aware, and able to admit our loss—we spend the second half trying to recover and reclaim the gift we once possessed.

When we lose track of true self, how can we pick up the trail? One way is to seek clues in stories from our younger years, years when we lived closer to our birthright gifts. A few years ago, I found some clues to myself in a time machine of sorts. A friend sent me a tattered copy of my high school newspaper from May 1957 in which I had been interviewed about what I intended to do with my life. With the certainty to be expected of a high school senior, I told the interviewer that I would become a naval aviator and then take up a career in advertising.

I was indeed "wearing other people's faces," and I can tell you exactly whose they were. My father worked with a man who had once been a navy pilot. He was Irish, charismatic, romantic, full of the wild blue yonder and a fair share of the blarney, and I wanted to be like him. The father of one of my boyhood friends was in advertising, and though I did not yearn to take on his persona, which was too buttoned-down for my taste, I did yearn for the fast car and other large toys that seemed to be the accessories of his selfhood!

These self-prophecies, now over forty years old, seem wildly misguided for a person who eventually became a Quaker, a would-be pacifist, a writer, and an activist. Taken literally, they illustrate how early in life we can lose track of who we are. But inspected through the lens of paradox, my desire to become an aviator and an advertiser contain clues to the core of true self that would take many years to emerge: clues, by definition, are coded and must be deciphered.

Hidden in my desire to become an "ad man" was a life-long fascination with language and its power to persuade, the same fascination that has kept me writing incessantly for decades. Hidden in my desire to become a naval aviator was something more complex: a personal engagement with the problem of violence that expressed itself at first in military fantasies and then, over a period of many years, resolved itself in the pacifism I aspire to today. When I flip the coin of identity I held to so tightly in high school, I find the paradoxical "opposite" that emerged as the years went by.

If I go farther back, to an earlier stage of my life, the clues need less deciphering to yield insight into my birthright gifts and callings. In grade school, I became fascinated with the mysteries of flight. As many boys did in those days, I spent endless hours, after school and on weekends, designing, crafting, flying, and (usually) crashing model airplanes made of fragile balsa wood.

Unlike most boys, however, I also spent long hours creating eight- and twelve-page books about aviation. I would turn a sheet of paper sideways; draw a vertical line down the middle; make diagrams of, say, the cross-section of a wing; roll the sheet into a typewriter; and peck out a caption explaining how air moving across an airfoil creates a vacuum that lifts the plane. Then I would fold that sheet in half along with several others I had made, staple the collection together down the spine, and painstakingly illustrate the cover.

I had always thought that the meaning of this paperwork was obvious: fascinated with flight, I wanted to be a pilot, or at least an aeronautical engineer. But recently, when I found a couple of these literary artifacts in an old cardboard box, I suddenly saw the truth, and it was more obvious than I had imagined. I didn't want to be a pilot or an aeronautical engineer or anything else related to aviation. I wanted to be an author, to make books—a task I have been attempting from the third grade to this very moment!

From the beginning, our lives lay down clues to selfhood and vocation, though the clues may be hard to decode. But trying to interpret them is profoundly worthwhile—especially when we are in our twenties or thirties or forties, feeling profoundly lost, having wandered, or been dragged, far away from our birthright gifts.

Those clues are helpful in counteracting the conventional concept of vocation, which insists that our lives must be driven by "oughts." As noble as that may sound, we do not find our callings by conforming ourselves to some abstract moral code. We find our callings by claiming authentic selfhood, by being who we are, by dwelling in the world as Zusya rather than straining to be Moses. The deepest vocational question is not "What ought I to do with my life?" It is the more elemental and demanding "Who am I? What is my nature?"

Everything in the universe has a nature, which means limits as well as potentials, a truth well known by people who work daily with the things of the world. Making pottery, for example, involves more than telling the clay what to become. The clay presses back on the potter's hands, telling her what it can and cannot do—and if she fails to listen, the outcome will be both frail and ungainly. Engineering involves more than telling materials what they must do. If the engineer does not honor the nature of the steel or the wood or the stone, his failure will go well beyond aesthetics: the bridge or the building will collapse and put human life in peril.

The human self also has a nature, limits as well as potentials. If you seek vocation without understanding the material you are working with, what you build with your life will be ungainly and may well put lives in peril, your own and some of those around you. "Faking it" in the service of high values is no virtue and has nothing to do with vocation. It is an ignorant, sometimes arrogant, attempt to override one's nature, and it will always fail.

Our deepest calling is to grow into our own authentic selfhood, whether or not it conforms to some image of who we *ought* to be. As we do so, we will not only find the joy that every human being seeks—we will also find our path of authentic service in the world. True vocation joins self and service, as Frederick Buechner asserts when he defines vocation as "the place where your deep gladness meets the world's deep need."[3]

Buechner's definition starts with the self and moves toward the needs of the world: it begins, wisely, where vocation begins—not in what the world needs (which is everything), but in the nature of the human self, in what brings the self joy, the deep joy of knowing that we are here on earth to be the gifts that God created.

Contrary to the conventions of our thinly moralistic culture, this emphasis on gladness and selfhood is not selfish. The Quaker teacher Douglas Steere was fond of saying that the ancient human question "Who am I?" leads inevitably to the equally important question "Whose am I?"—for there is no selfhood outside of relationship. We must ask the question of selfhood and answer it as honestly as we can, no matter where it takes us. Only as we do so can we discover the community of our lives.

As I learn more about the seed of true self that was planted when I was born, I also learn more about the ecosystem in which I was planted—the network of communal relations in which I am called to live responsively, accountably, and joyfully with beings of every sort. Only when I know both seed and system, self and community, can I embody the great commandment to love both my neighbor and myself.

JOURNEY INTO DARKNESS

Most of us arrive at a sense of self and vocation only after a long journey through alien lands. But this journey bears no resemblance to the trouble-free "travel packages" sold by the tourism industry. It is more akin to the ancient tradition of pilgrimage—"a transformative journey to a sacred center" full of hardships, darkness, and peril.[4]

In the tradition of pilgrimage, those hardships are seen not as accidental but as integral to the journey itself. Treacherous terrain, bad weather, taking a fall, getting lost—challenges of that sort, largely beyond our control, can strip the ego of the illusion that it is in charge and make space for true self to emerge. If that happens, the pilgrim has a better chance to find the sacred center he or she seeks. Disabused of our illusions by much travel and travail, we awaken one day to find that the sacred center is here and now—in every moment of the journey, everywhere in the world around us, and deep within our own hearts.

But before we come to that center, full of light, we must travel in the dark. Darkness is not the whole of the story—every pilgrimage has passages of loveliness and joy—but it is the part of the story most often left untold. When we finally escape the darkness and stumble into the light, it is tempting to tell others that our hope never flagged, to deny those long nights we spent cowering in fear.

The experience of darkness has been essential to my coming into selfhood, and telling the truth about that fact helps me stay in the light. But I want to tell that truth for another reason as well: many young people today journey in the dark, as the young always have, and we elders do them a disservice when we withhold the shadowy parts of our lives. When I was young, there were very few elders willing to talk about the darkness; most of them pretended that success was all they had ever known. As the darkness began to descend on me in my early twenties, I thought I had developed a unique and terminal case of failure. I did not realize that I had merely embarked on a journey toward joining the human race.

The story of my journey is no more or less important than anyone else's. It is simply the best source of data I have on a subject where generalizations often fail but truth may be found in the details. I want to rehearse a few details of my travels, and travails, extracting some insights about vocation as I go. I do so partly as an offering of honesty to the young and partly as a reminder to anyone who needs it that the nuances of personal experience contain much guidance toward self-hood and vocation.

My journey into darkness began in sunlit places. I grew up in a Chicago suburb and went to Carleton College in Minnesota, a splendid place where I found new faces to wear—faces more like my own than the ones I donned in high school, but still the faces of other people. Wearing one of them, I went from college neither to the navy nor to Madison Avenue but to Union Theological Seminary in New York City, as certain that the ministry was now my calling as I had been a few years earlier about advertising and aviation.

So it came as a great shock when, at the end of my first year, God spoke to me—in the form of mediocre grades and massive misery—and informed me that under no conditions was I to become an ordained leader in His or Her church. Always responsive to authority, as one was if raised in the fifties, I left Union and went west, to the University of California at Berkeley. There I spent much of the sixties working on a Ph.D. in sociology and learning to be not quite so responsive to authority.

Berkeley in the sixties was, of course, an astounding mix of shadow and light. But contrary to the current myth, many of us were less seduced by the shadow than drawn by the light, coming away from that time and place with a lifelong sense of hope, a feeling for community, a passion for social change.

Though I taught for two years in the middle of graduate school, discovering that I loved teaching and was good at it, my Berkeley experience left me convinced that a university career would be a cop-out. I felt called instead to work on "the urban crisis." So when I left Berkeley in the late sixties— a friend kept asking me, "Why do you want to go back to America?"—I also left academic life. Indeed, I left on a white horse (some might say a high horse), full of righteous indignation about the academy's corruption, holding aloft the flaming sword of truth. I moved to Washington, D.C., where I became not a professor but a community organizer.

What I learned about the world from that work was the subject of an earlier book.[5] What I learned about vocation is how one's values can do battle with one's heart. I felt morally compelled to work on the urban crisis, but doing so went against a growing sense that teaching might be my vocation. My heart wanted to keep teaching, but my ethics—laced liberally with ego—told me I was supposed to save the city. How could I reconcile the contradiction between the two?

After two years of community organizing, with all its financial uncertainties, Georgetown University offered me a faculty post—one that did not require me to get off my white horse altogether: "We don't want you to be on campus all week long," said the dean. "We want you to get our students involved in the community. Here's a tenure-track position involving a minimum of classes and no requirement to serve on committees. Keep working in the community and take our students out there with you."

The part about no committees seemed like a gift from God, so I accepted Georgetown's offer and began involving undergraduates in community organizing. But I soon found an even bigger gift hidden in this arrangement. By looking anew at my community work through the lens of education, I saw that as an organizer I had never stopped being a teacher— I was simply teaching in a classroom without walls.

In fact, I could have done no other: teaching, I was coming to understand, is my native way of being in the world. Make me a cleric or a CEO, a poet or a politico, and teaching is what I will do. Teaching is at the heart of my vocation and will manifest itself in any role I play. Georgetown's invitation allowed me to take my first step toward embracing this truth, toward a lifelong exploration of "education unplugged."

But even this way of reframing my work could not alter the fact that there was a fundamental misfit between the rough-and-tumble of organizing and my own overly sensitive nature. After five years of conflict and competition, I burned out. I was too thin-skinned to make a good community organizer — my vocational reach had exceeded my grasp. I had been driven more by the "oughts" of the urban crisis than by a sense of true self. Lacking insight into my own limits and potentials, I had allowed ego and ethics to lead me into a situation that my soul could not abide.

I was disappointed in myself for not being tough enough to take the flak, disappointed and ashamed. But as pilgrims must discover if they are to complete their quest, we are led to truth by our weaknesses as well as our strengths. I needed to leave community organizing for a reason I might never have acknowledged had I not been thin-skinned and burned-out: as an organizer, I was trying to take people to a place where I had never been myself — a place called community. If I wanted to do community-related work with integrity, I needed a deeper immersion in community than I had experienced to that point.

I am white, middle-class, and male — not exactly a leading candidate for a communal life. People like me are raised to live autonomously, not interdependently. I had been trained to compete and win, and I had developed a taste for the prizes. But something in me yearned to experience communion, not competition, and that something might never have made itself known had burnout not forced me to seek another way.

So I took a yearlong sabbatical from my work in Washington and went to a place called Pendle Hill outside of Philadelphia. Founded in 1930, Pendle Hill is a Quaker living-and-learning community of some seventy people whose mission is to offer education about the inner journey, nonviolent social change, and the connection between the two. It is a real-time experiment in Quaker faith and practice where residents move through a daily round of communal life: worshiping in silence each morning; sharing three meals a day; engaging in study, physical work, decision making, and social outreach. It is a commune, an ashram, a monastery, a zendo, a kibbutz—whatever one calls it, Pendle Hill was a life unlike anything I had ever known.[6]

Moving there was like moving to Mars—utterly alien but profoundly compelling. I thought I would stay for just a year and then go back to Washington and resume my work. But before my sabbatical ended, I was invited to become Pendle Hill's dean of studies. I stayed on for another decade, living in community and continuing my experiment with alternative models of education.

It was a transformative passage for me, personally, professionally, and spiritually; in retrospect, I know how impoverished I would have been without it. But early on in that passage I began to have deep and painful doubts about the trajectory of my vocation. Though I felt called to stay at Pendle Hill, I also feared that I had stepped off the edge of the known world and was at risk of disappearing professionally.

From high school on, I had been surrounded by expectations that I would ascend to some sort of major leadership. When I was twenty-nine, the president of a prestigious college visited me in Berkeley to recruit me for his board of trustees. He was doing it, he joked, because no one on that board was under sixty, let alone thirty; worse still, not one of them had a beard, which I could supply as part of the Berkeley uniform. Then he added, "In fact, I'm doing this because some day you'll be a college president—of that I'm sure—and serving as a trustee is an important part of your apprenticeship." I accepted his invitation because I felt certain that he was right.

So half a dozen years later, what was I doing at Pendle Hill, a "commune" known to few, run by an offbeat religious community that most people can identify only by their oatmeal—which, I hasten to add, is not really made by Quakers?

I'll tell you what I was doing: I was in the craft shop making mugs that weighed more and looked worse than the clay ashtrays I made in grade school, and I was sending these monstrosities home as gifts to my family. My father, rest his soul, was in the fine chinaware business, and I was sending him mugs so heavy you could fill them with coffee and not feel any difference in weight!

Family and friends were asking me—and I was asking myself—"Why did you get a Ph.D. if this is what you are going to do? Aren't you squandering your opportunities and gifts?" Under that sort of scrutiny, my vocational decision felt wasteful and ridiculous; what's more, it was terrifying to an ego like mine that had no desire to disappear and every desire to succeed and become well known.

Did I *want* to go to Pendle Hill, to be at Pendle Hill, to stay at Pendle Hill? I cannot say that I did. But I can say with certainty that Pendle Hill was something that I *couldn't not do.*

Vocation at its deepest level is not, "Oh, boy, do I want to go to this strange place where I have to learn a new way to live and where no one, including me, understands what I'm doing." Vocation at its deepest level is, "This is something I can't not do, for reasons I'm unable to explain to anyone else and don't fully understand myself but that are nonetheless compelling."

And yet, even with this level of motivation, my doubts multiplied. One day I walked from Pendle Hill through the woods to a nearby college campus, out for a simple stroll but carrying my anxiety with me. On some forgotten whim, I went into the college's main administration building. There, in the foyer, hung several stern portraits of past presidents of that institution. One of them was the same man who, as president of another institution, had come out to Berkeley to recruit me for his board of trustees—a man who, in my imagination, was now staring down at me with a deeply disapproving look on his face: "What do you think you're up to? Why are you wasting your time? Get back on track before it is too late!"

I ran from that building back into the woods and wept for a long time. Perhaps this moment precipitated the descent into darkness that has been so central to my vocational journey, a descent that hit bottom in the struggle with clinical depression that I will write about later in this book. But whether that is the case or not, the moment was large with things I needed to learn—and could learn only by going into the dark.

In that moment, all the false bravado about why I had left academic life collapsed around me, and I was left with nothing more than the reality of my own fear. I had insisted, to myself as well as others, that I wanted out of the university because it was unfit for human habitation. It was, I argued, a place of corruption and arrogance, filled with intellectuals who evaded their social responsibilities and yet claimed superiority over ordinary folks—the very folks whose lack of power and privilege compelled them to shoulder the responsibilities that kept our society intact.

If those complaints sound unoriginal, it is only because they are. They were the accepted pieties of Berkeley in the sixties, which—for reasons I now understand—I eagerly embraced as my own. Whatever half-truths about the university my complaints may have contained, they served me primarily as a misleading and self-serving explanation of why I fled academic life.

The truth is that I fled because I was afraid—afraid that I could never succeed as a scholar, afraid that I could never measure up to the university's standards for research and publication. And I was right—though it took many years before I could admit that to myself. Try as I may, try as I might, I have never had the gifts that make for a good scholar—and remaining in the university would have been a distorting denial of that fact.

A scholar is committed to building on knowledge that others have gathered, correcting it, confirming it, enlarging it. But I have always wanted to think my own thoughts about a subject without being overly influenced by what others have thought before me. If you catch me reading a book in private, it is most likely to be a novel, some poetry, a mystery, or an essay that defies classification, rather than a text directly related to whatever I am writing at the time.

There is some virtue in my proclivities, I think: they help me keep my thinking fresh and bring me the stimulation that comes from looking at life through multiple lenses. There is non-virtue in them as well: laziness of a sort, a certain kind of impatience, and perhaps even a lack of due respect for others who have worked these fields.

But be they virtues or faults, these are the simple facts about my nature, about my limits and my gifts. I am less gifted at building on other people's discoveries than at tinkering in my own garage; less gifted at slipping slowly into a subject than at jumping into the deep end to see if I can swim; less gifted at making outlines than at writing myself into a corner and trying to find a way out; less gifted at tracking a tight chain of logic than at leaping from one metaphor to the next!

Perhaps there is a lesson here about the complexity, even duplicity, we must embrace on the road to vocation, where we sometimes find ourselves needing to do the right thing for the wrong reason. It was right for me to leave the university. But I needed to do it for the wrong reason—"the university is corrupt"—because the right reason—"I lack the gifts of a scholar"—was too frightening for me to face at the time.

My fear of failing as a scholar contained the energy I needed to catapult myself out of the academy and free myself for another kind of educational mission. But because I could not acknowledge my fear, I had to disguise that energy as the white horse of judgment and self-righteousness. It is an awkward fact, but it is true—and once I could acknowledge that truth and understand its role in the dynamics of my life, I found myself no longer embarrassed by it.

Eventually, I was able to get off that white horse and take an unblinking look at myself and my liabilities. This was a step into darkness that I had been trying to avoid—the darkness of seeing myself more honestly than I really wanted to. But I am grateful for the grace that allowed me to dismount, for the white horse I was riding back then could never have carried me to the place where I am today: serving, with love, the academy I once left in fear and loathing.

Today I serve education from outside the institution—where my pathology is less likely to get triggered—rather than from the inside, where I waste energy on anger instead of investing it in hope. This pathology, which took me years to recognize, is my tendency to get so conflicted with the way people use power in institutions that I spend more time being angry at them than I spend on my real work.

Once I understood that the problem was "in here" as well as "out there," the solution seemed clear: I needed to work independently, outside of institutions, detached from the stimuli that trigger my knee-jerk response. Having done just that for over a decade now, my pathology no longer troubles me: I have no one to blame but myself for whatever the trouble may be and am compelled to devote my energies to the work I am called to do!

Here, I think, is another clue to finding true self and vocation: we must withdraw the negative projections we make on people and situations—projections that serve mainly to mask our fears about ourselves—and acknowledge and embrace our own liabilities and limits.

Once I came to terms with my fears, I was able to look back and trace an unconscious pattern. For years, I had been moving away from large institutions like Berkeley and Georgetown to small places like Pendle Hill, places of less status and visibility on the map of social reality. But I moved like a crab, sideways, too fearful to look head-on at the fact that I was taking myself from the center to the fringes of institutional life— and ultimately to a place where all that was left was to move outside of institutions altogether.

I rationalized my movement with the notion that small institutions are more moral than large ones. But that is patently untrue—both about what was animating me and about institutions! In fact, I was animated by a soul, a "true self," that knew me better than my ego did, knew that I needed to work outside of institutional crosscurrents and constraints.

This is not an indictment of institutions; it is a statement of my limitations. Among my admired friends are people who do not have my limits, whose gifts allow them to work faithfully within institutions and, through those institutions, to serve the world well. But their gift is not mine, as I learned after much *Sturm und Drang*—and that is not an indictment of me. It is simply a truth about who I am and how I am rightfully related to the world, an ecological truth of the sort that can point toward true vocation.

SELFHOOD, SOCIETY, AND SERVICE

By surviving passages of doubt and depression on the vocational journey, I have become clear about at least one thing: self-care is never a selfish act—it is simply good stewardship of the only gift I have, the gift I was put on earth to offer to others. Anytime we can listen to true self and give it the care it requires, we do so not only for ourselves but for the many others whose lives we touch.

There are at least two ways to understand the link between selfhood and service. One is offered by the poet Rumi in his piercing observation: "If you are here unfaithfully with us, you're causing terrible damage."[7] If we are unfaithful to true self, we will extract a price from others. We will make promises we cannot keep, build houses from flimsy stuff, conjure dreams that devolve into nightmares, and other people will suffer—if we are unfaithful to true self.

I will examine that sort of unfaithfulness, and its consequences, later in this book. But a more inspiring way of understanding the link between selfhood and service is to study the lives of people who have been here *faithfully* with us. Look, for example, at the great liberation movements that have served humanity so well—in eastern Europe, Latin America, and South Africa, among women, African Americans, and our gay and lesbian brothers and sisters. What we see is simple but often ignored: the movements that transform us, our relations, and our world emerge from the lives of people who decide to care for their authentic selfhood.

The social systems in which these people must survive often try to force them to live in a way untrue to who they are. If you are poor, you are supposed to accept, with gratitude, half a loaf or less; if you are black, you are supposed to suffer racism without protest; if you are gay, you are supposed to pretend that you are not. You and I may not know, but we can at least imagine, how tempting it would be to mask one's truth in situations of this sort—because the system threatens punishment if one does not.

But in spite of that threat, or because of it, the people who plant the seeds of movements make a critical decision: they decide to live "divided no more." *They decide no longer to act on the outside in a way that contradicts some truth about themselves that they hold deeply on the inside.* They decide to claim authentic selfhood and act it out—and their decisions ripple out to transform the society in which they live, serving the selfhood of millions of others.

I call this the "Rosa Parks decision" because that remarkable woman is so emblematic of what the undivided life can mean. Most of us know her story, the story of an African American woman who, at the time she made her decision, was a seamstress in her early forties. On December 1, 1955, in Montgomery, Alabama, Rosa Parks did something she was not supposed to do: she sat down at the front of a bus in one of the seats reserved for whites—a dangerous, daring, and provocative act in a racist society.

Legend has it that years later a graduate student came to Rosa Parks and asked, "Why did you sit down at the front of the bus that day?" Rosa Parks did not say that she sat down to launch a movement, because her motives were more elemental than that. She said, "I sat down because I was tired." But she did not mean that her feet were tired. She meant that her soul was tired, her heart was tired, her whole being was tired of playing by racist rules, of denying her soul's claim to selfhood.[8]

Of course, there were many forces aiding and abetting Rosa Parks's decision to live divided no more. She had studied the theory and tactics of nonviolence at the Highlander Folk School, where Martin Luther King Jr. was also a student. She was secretary of the Montgomery chapter of the National Association for the Advancement of Colored People, whose members had been discussing civil disobedience.

But in the moment she sat down at the front of the bus on that December day, she had no guarantee that the theory of nonviolence would work or that her community would back her up. It was a moment of existential truth, of claiming authentic selfhood, of reclaiming birthright giftedness—and in that moment she set in motion a process that changed both the lay and the law of the land.

Rosa Parks sat down because she had reached a point where it was essential to embrace her true vocation—not as someone who would reshape our society but as someone who would live out her full self in the world. She decided, "I will no longer act on the outside in a way that contradicts the truth that I hold deeply on the inside. I will no longer act as if I were less than the whole person I know myself inwardly to be."

Where does one get the courage to "sit down at the front of the bus" in a society that punishes anyone who decides to live divided no more? After all, conventional wisdom recommends the divided life as the safe and sane way to go: "Don't wear your heart on your sleeve." "Don't make a federal case out of it." "Don't show them the whites of your eyes." These are all the clichéd ways we tell each other to keep personal truth apart from public life, lest we make ourselves vulnerable in that rough-and-tumble realm.

Where do people find the courage to live divided no more when they know they will be punished for it? The answer I have seen in the lives of people like Rosa Parks is simple: these people have transformed the notion of punishment itself. They have come to understand that *no punishment anyone might inflict on them could possibly be worse than the punishment they inflict on themselves by conspiring in their own diminishment.*

In the Rosa Parks story, that insight emerges in a wonderful way. After she had sat at the front of the bus for a while, the police came aboard and said, "You know, if you continue to sit there, we're going to have to throw you in jail."

Rosa Parks replied, "You may do that . . .," which is a very polite way of saying, "What could your jail of stone and steel possibly mean to me, compared to the self-imposed imprisonment I've suffered for forty years—the prison I've just walked out of by refusing to conspire any longer with this racist system?"

The punishment imposed on us for claiming true self can never be worse than the punishment we impose on ourselves by failing to make that claim. And the converse is true as well: no reward anyone might give us could possibly be greater than the reward that comes from living by our own best lights.

You and I may not have Rosa Parks's particular battle to fight, the battle with institutional racism. The universal element in her story is not the substance of her fight but the selfhood in which she stood while she fought it—for each of us holds the challenge and the promise of naming and claiming true self.

But if the Rosa Parks story is to help us discern our own vocations, we must see her as the ordinary person she is. That will be difficult to do because we have made her into superwoman—and we have done it to protect ourselves. If we can keep Rosa Parks in a museum as an untouchable icon of truth, we will remain untouchable as well: we can put her up on a pedestal and praise her, world without end, never finding ourselves challenged by her life.

Since my own life runs no risk of being displayed in a museum case, I want to return briefly to the story I know best—my own. Unlike Rosa Parks, I never took a singular, dramatic action that might create the energy of transformation around the institutions I care about. Instead, I tried to abandon those institutions through an evasive, crablike movement that I did not want to acknowledge, even to myself.

But a funny thing happened on the way to my vocation. Today, twenty-five years after I left education in anger and fear, my work is deeply related to the renewal of educational institutions. I believe that this is possible only because my true self dragged me, kicking and screaming, toward honoring its nature and needs, forcing me to find my rightful place in the ecosystem of life, to find a right relation to institutions with which I have a lifelong lover's quarrel. Had I denied my true self, remaining "at my post" simply because I was paralyzed with fear, I would almost certainly be lost in bitterness today instead of serving a cause I care about.

Rosa Parks took her stand with clarity and courage. I took mine by diversion and default. Some journeys are direct, and some are circuitous; some are heroic, and some are fearful and muddled. But every journey, honestly undertaken, stands a chance of taking us toward the place where our deep gladness meets the world's deep need.

As May Sarton reminds us, the pilgrimage toward true self will take "time, many years and places." The world needs people with the patience and the passion to make that pilgrimage not only for their own sake but also as a social and political act. The world still waits for the truth that will set us free—my truth, your truth, our truth—the truth that was seeded in the earth when each of us arrived here formed in the image of God. Cultivating that truth, I believe, is the authentic vocation of every human being.

CHAPTER III

When Way Closes

WAY WILL OPEN

By the time I began my sabbatical at Pendle Hill—the year that stretched into a decade—I had been in Washington, D.C., for five years, growing more fearful every day that I was living a life not my own. I was thirty-five years old and had a Ph.D. and decent references, so finding a new job would have been no great problem, not in that place and time. But I wanted more than a job. I wanted deeper congruence between my inner and outer life.

I had worked in Washington as both a community organizer and a professor, an activist and an intellectual—without feeling at home in either of those worlds. If you buy the scurrilous notion that "those who can, do, and those who can't, teach" (which I may have half-believed at the time, mired as I was in a slough of despond) you will understand why it felt like I had exhausted all possible vocations!

If I were ever to discover a new direction, I thought, it would be at Pendle Hill, a community rooted in prayer, study, and a vision of human possibility. But when I arrived and started sharing my vocational quandary, people responded with a traditional Quaker counsel that, despite their good intentions, left me even more discouraged. "Have faith," they said, "and *way will open*."

"I have faith," I thought to myself. "What I don't have is time to wait for 'way' to open. I'm approaching middle age at warp speed, and I have yet to find a vocational path that feels right. The only way that's opened so far is the wrong way."

After a few months of deepening frustration, I took my troubles to an older Quaker woman well known for her thoughtfulness and candor. "Ruth," I said, "people keep telling me that 'way will open.' Well, I sit in the silence, I pray, I listen for my calling, but way is not opening. I've been trying to find my vocation for a long time, and I still don't have the foggiest idea of what I'm meant to do. Way may open for other people, but it's sure not opening for me."

Ruth's reply was a model of Quaker plain-speaking. "I'm a birthright Friend," she said somberly, "and in sixty-plus years of living, way has never opened in front of me." She paused, and I started sinking into despair. Was this wise woman telling me that the Quaker concept of God's guidance was a hoax?

Then she spoke again, this time with a grin. "But a lot of way has closed behind me, and that's had the same guiding effect."

I laughed with her, laughed loud and long, the kind of laughter that comes when a simple truth exposes your heart for the needlessly neurotic mess it has become. Ruth's honesty gave me a new way to look at my vocational journey, and my experience has long since confirmed the lesson she taught me that day: there is as much guidance in what does not and cannot happen in my life as there is in what can and does—maybe more.

Like many middle-class Americans, especially those who are white and male, I was raised in a subculture that insisted I could do anything I wanted to do, be anything I wanted to be, if I were willing to make the effort. The message was that both the universe and I were without limits, given enough energy and commitment on my part. God made things that way, and all I had to do was to get with the program.

My troubles began, of course, when I started to slam into my limitations, especially in the form of failure. I can still touch the shame I felt when, in the summer before I started graduate school at Berkeley, I experienced my first serious comeuppance: I was fired from my research assistantship in sociology.

Having been a golden boy through grade school, high school, and college, I was devastated by this sudden turn of fate. Not only was my source of summer income gone, but my entire graduate career seemed in jeopardy; the professor I had come to Berkeley to study with was the director of the project from which I had been fired. My sense of identity, and my concept of the universe, crumbled around my feet for the first, but not last, time. What had happened to my limitless self in a limitless world?

The culture I was raised in suggested an answer: I had not worked hard enough at my job to keep it, let alone succeed. I regret to report that there is some truth in that answer. Another research assistant and I had made frequent, disrespectful, and (apparently) audible jokes about the project on which we were working. We goofed off so much that our supervisor got bent out of shape, as perhaps did some of the data we were punching into IBM counter-sorter cards.

My associate and I had rationalized our behavior with the juvenile notion that the project was a joke long before we started making jokes about it. Today, thirty years later, my inner adolescent—which is less wise but more tenacious than the infamous "inner child"—still clings to the belief that we may well have been right! Whatever merit this twisted rationale may have, it is true that I did not work hard enough to keep that job, and so I lost it.

LEARNING OUR LIMITS

But that truth does not go deep enough—not if I am to discover the meaning of "way closing" behind me. I was fired because that job had little or nothing to do with who I am, with my true nature and gifts, with what I care and do not care about. My resort to adolescent rebellion reflected that simple fact.

I apologize, belatedly, for my immaturity, for the grief I gave my supervisor, and for whatever damage I may have done to the data. None of that is to my credit. But I was laughing to keep myself sane. Perhaps the research I was doing was what a good sociologist "ought" to do, but it felt meaningless to me, and I felt fraudulent doing it. Those feelings were harbingers of things to come, things that eventually led me out of the profession altogether.

Obviously, I should have dealt with my feelings more directly and exercised more self-control. Either I should have quit that job under my own steam or settled in and done the work properly. But sometimes the "shoulds" do not work because the life one is living runs crosswise to the grain of one's soul. At that time in my life, I had no feeling for the grain of my soul and no sense of which way was crosswise. Not knowing what was driving me, I behaved with blind but blissful unconsciousness—and reality responded by giving me a big and hard-to-take clue about who I am: way closed behind me.

Neither that job nor any job like it was in the cards for me, given the hand I was dealt at birth. That may sound like sinfully fatalistic thinking or, worse, a self-serving excuse. But I believe it embodies a simple, healthy, and life-giving truth about vocation. Each of us arrives here with a nature, which means both limits and potentials. We can learn as much about our nature by running into our limits as by experiencing our potentials. That, I think, is what Ruth and life were trying to teach me.

It would be nice if our limits did not reveal themselves in such embarrassing ways as getting fired from a job. But if you are like me and don't readily admit your limits, embarrassment may be the only way to get your attention. I go on full alert only when I am blocked or get derailed or flat-out fail. Then, finally, I may be forced to face my nature and find out whether I can make something of both my gifts and my limitations.

It is important to distinguish between two kinds of limitations: those that come with selfhood and those that are imposed by people or political forces hell-bent on keeping us "in our place." I do not ask everyone who gets fired to conclude that it was the work of a gracious God offering clues to one's true vocation. Sometimes it is the work of a pathological boss or a corporate culture, getting rid of people whose propensity for truth-telling threatens the status quo. Sometimes it is the result of an economic system that robs the poor of their jobs so that the rich can get richer still. Like everything else in the spiritual life, getting guidance from way closing requires thoughtful discernment.

Our problem as Americans—at least, among my race and gender—is that we resist the very idea of limits, regarding limits of all sorts as temporary and regrettable impositions on our lives. Our national myth is about the endless defiance of limits: opening the western frontier, breaking the speed of sound, dropping people on the moon, discovering "cyberspace" at the very moment when we have filled old-fashioned space with so much junk that we can barely move. We refuse to take no for an answer.

Part of me treasures the hopefulness of this American legacy. But when I consistently refuse to take no for an answer, I miss the vital clues to my identity that arise when way closes—and I am more likely both to exceed my limits and to do harm to others in the process.

A few years ago, I was introduced at a conference as a "recovering sociologist." The line got a good laugh, but it also snapped me back to my ignominious failure in the summer before I began graduate school. My soul needed to recover from the misfit between sociology and itself. But before that could happen, my ego needed to deal with its shame. I had to get through graduate school and prove, however briefly, that I could succeed as a professor of sociology—even though that path took me directly into vocational despair.

The despair that took me from teaching sociology at Georgetown to the community at Pendle Hill contained a call to vocational integrity. Had I not followed my despair, and had Ruth not helped me understand it, I might have continued to pursue a work that was not mine to do, causing further harm to myself, to the people and projects with which I worked, and to a profession that is well worth doing—by those who are called to do it.

THE ECOLOGY OF A LIFE

Despite the American myth, I cannot be or do whatever I desire—a truism, to be sure, but a truism we often defy. Our created natures make us like organisms in an ecosystem: there are some roles and relationships in which we thrive and others in which we wither and die.

It is clear, for example, as I enter my sixties, that I cannot and will not be president of the United States, even though I grew up surrounded by a rhetoric that said that anyone (read "any white male") could rise to that lofty role. I no longer grieve this particular limitation, for I cannot imagine a crueler fate for someone with my nature than to be president of *anything*, let alone a nation-state. Still, encouraged by the myth of the limitless self, I spent many years trying to deny this ecological truth. Here is a story to prove it.

During my tenure as dean at Pendle Hill, I was offered the opportunity to become the president of a small educational institution. I had visited the campus; spoken with trustees, administrators, faculty, and students; and had been told that if I wanted it, the job was most likely mine.

Vexed as I was about vocation, I was quite certain that this was the job for me. So as is the custom in the Quaker community, I called on half a dozen trusted friends to help me discern my vocation by means of a "clearness committee," a process in which the group refrains from giving you advice but spends three hours asking you honest, open questions to help you discover your own inner truth.[1] (Looking back, of course, it is clear that my real intent in convening this group was not to discern anything but to brag about being offered a job I had already decided to accept!)

For a while, the questions were easy, at least for a dreamer like me: What is your vision for this institution? What is its mission in the larger society? How would you change the curriculum? How would you handle decision making? What about dealing with conflict?

Halfway into the process, someone asked a question that sounded easier yet but turned out to be very hard: "What would you like most about being a president?"

The simplicity of that question loosed me from my head and lowered me into my heart. I remember pondering for at least a full minute before I could respond. Then, very softly and tentatively, I started to speak: "Well, I would not like having to give up my writing and my teaching. . . . I would not like the politics of the presidency, never knowing who your real friends are. . . . I would not like having to glad-hand people I do not respect simply because they have money. . . . I would not like . . ."

Gently but firmly, the person who had posed the question interrupted me: "May I remind you that I asked what you would most *like*?"

I responded impatiently, "Yes, yes, I'm working my way toward an answer." Then I resumed my sullen but honest litany: "I would not like having to give up my summer vacations. . . . I would not like having to wear a suit and tie all the time. . . . I would not like . . ."

Once again the questioner called me back to the original question. But this time I felt compelled to give the only honest answer I possessed, an answer that came from the very bottom of my barrel, an answer that appalled even me as I spoke it.

"Well," said I, in the smallest voice I possess, "I guess what I'd like most is getting my picture in the paper with the word *president* under it."

I was sitting with seasoned Quakers who knew that though my answer was laughable, my mortal soul was clearly at stake! They did not laugh at all but went into a long and serious silence—a silence in which I could only sweat and inwardly groan.

Finally my questioner broke the silence with a question that cracked all of us up—and cracked me open: "Parker," he said, "can you think of an easier way to get your picture in the paper?"

By then it was obvious, even to me, that my desire to be president had much more to do with my ego than with the ecology of my life—so obvious that when the clearness committee ended, I called the school and withdrew my name from consideration. Had I taken that job, it would have been very bad for me and a disaster for the school.

The ecological theory of life, the theory of limits, works wonderfully well with situations like this: my nature makes me unfit to be president of anything, and therefore—if I stay true to what I know about myself—I will die having avoided a fate that for me would be worse than death.

But what happens to the theory of limits when what I want to do is not to get my picture in the paper but to meet some human need? What happens to that theory when my vocational motive is virtuous, not egotistical: to be a teacher from whom students can learn or a counselor who helps people find themselves or an activist who sets injustice right? Unfortunately, the theory of limits can work as powerfully in these cases as it does with my presidential prospects. There are some things I "ought" to do or be that are simply beyond my reach.

If I try to be or do something noble that has nothing to do with who I am, I may look good to others and to myself for a while. But the fact that I am exceeding my limits will eventually have consequences. I will distort myself, the other, and our relationship—and may end up doing more damage than if I had never set out to do this particular "good." When I try to do something that is not in my nature or the nature of the relationship, way will close behind me.

Here is one example of what I mean. Over the years, I have met people who have made a very human claim on me by making known their need to be loved. For a long time, my response was instant and reflexive, born of the "oughts" I had absorbed: "Of course you need to be loved. Everyone does. And I love you."

It took me a long time to understand that although everyone needs to be loved, I cannot be the source of that gift to everyone who asks me for it. There are some relations in which I am capable of love and others in which I am not. To pretend otherwise, to put out promissory notes I am unable to honor, is to damage my own integrity and that of the person in need—all in the name of love.

Here is another example of violating one's nature in the name of nobility, an example that shows the larger dangers of false love. Years ago, I heard Dorothy Day speak. Founder of the Catholic Worker movement, her long-term commitment to living among the poor on New York's Lower East Side—not just serving them but sharing their condition—had made her one of my heroes. So it came as a great shock when in the middle of her talk, I heard her start to ruminate about the "ungrateful poor."

I did not understand how such a dismissive phrase could come from the lips of a saint—until it hit me with the force of a Zen koan. Dorothy Day was saying, "Do not give to the poor expecting to get their gratitude so that you can feel good about yourself. If you do, your giving will be thin and short-lived, and that is not what the poor need; it will only impoverish them further. Give only if you have something you must give; give only if you are someone for whom giving is its own reward."

When I give something I do not possess, I give a false and dangerous gift, a gift that looks like love but is, in reality, loveless—a gift given more from my need to prove myself than from the other's need to be cared for. That kind of giving is not only loveless but faithless, based on the arrogant and mistaken notion that God has no way of channeling love to the other except through me. Yes, we are created in and for community, to be there, in love, for one another. But community cuts both ways: when we reach the limits of our own capacity to love, community means trusting that someone else will be available to the person in need.

One sign that I am violating my own nature in the name of nobility is a condition called burnout. Though usually regarded as the result of trying to give too much, burnout in my experience results from trying to give what I do not possess — the ultimate in giving too little! Burnout is a state of emptiness, to be sure, but it does not result from giving all I have: it merely reveals the nothingness from which I was trying to give in the first place.

May Sarton, in her poem "Now I Become Myself," uses images from the natural world to describe a different kind of giving, grounded in a different way of being, a way that results not in burnout but in fecundity and abundance:

> As slowly as the ripening fruit
> Fertile, detached, and always spent,
> Falls but does not exhaust the root . . .[2]

When the gift I give to the other is integral to my own nature, when it comes from a place of organic reality within me, it will renew itself—and me—even as I give it away. Only

when I give something that does not grow within me do I
deplete myself and harm the other as well, for only harm can
come from a gift that is forced, inorganic, unreal.

THE GOD OF REALITY

The God I know does not ask us to conform to some abstract
norm for the ideal self. God asks us only to honor our created
nature, which means our limits as well as potentials. When we
fail to do so, reality happens—God happens—and way closes
behind us.

The God I was told about in church, and still hear about
from time to time, runs about like an anxious schoolmaster
measuring people's behavior with a moral yardstick. But the
God I know is the source of reality rather than morality, the
source of what *is* rather than what *ought to be.* This does not
mean that God has nothing to do with morality: morality and
its consequences are built into the God-given structure of reality itself. Moral norms are not something we have to stretch
for, and moral consequences are not something we have to
wait for: they are right here, right now, waiting for us to honor,
or violate, the nature of self, other, world.

The attempt to live by the reality of our own nature, which
means our limits as well as our potentials, is a profoundly
moral regimen. John Middleton Murry put this truth into

words that challenge the conventional concept of goodness to its core: "For a good man to realize that it is better to be whole than to be good is to enter on a strait and narrow path compared to which his previous rectitude was flowery license."[3]

The God whom I know dwells quietly in the root system of the very nature of things. This is the God who, when asked by Moses for a name, responded, "I Am who I Am" (Exodus 3:14), an answer that has less to do with the moral rules for which Moses made God famous than with elemental "isness" and selfhood. If, as I believe, we are all made in God's image, we could all give the same answer when asked who we are: "I Am who I Am." One dwells with God by being faithful to one's nature. One crosses God by trying to be something one is not. Reality—including one's own—is divine, to be not defied but honored.

Lest this theologizing become too ethereal, I want to give an example of how honoring one's created nature can support morality in practice. I sometimes lead workshops for teachers who want to become better at their craft. At a certain point, I ask them to write brief descriptions of two recent moments in the classroom: a moment when things went so well that you knew you were born to be a teacher *and* a moment when things went so poorly that you wished you had never been born!

Then we get into small groups to learn more about our own natures through the two cases. First, I ask people to help each other identify the gifts that they possess that made the good moment possible. It is an affirming experience to see our gifts at work in a real-life situation—and it often takes the eyes of others to help us see. Our strongest gifts are usually those we are barely aware of possessing. They are a part of our God-given nature, with us from the moment we drew first breath, and we are no more conscious of having them than we are of breathing.

Then we turn to the second case. Having been bathed with praise in the first case, people now expect to be subjected to analysis, critique, and a variety of fixes: "If I had been in your shoes, I would have . . . ," or, "Next time you are in a situation like that, why don't you . . . ?" But I ask them to avoid that approach. I ask them instead to help each other see how limitations and liabilities are the flip side of our gifts, how a particular weakness is the inevitable trade-off for a particular strength. We will become better teachers not by trying to fill the potholes in our souls but by knowing them so well that we can avoid falling into them.

My gift as a teacher is the ability to "dance" with my students, to teach and learn with them through dialogue and interaction. When my students are willing to dance with me, the result can be a thing of beauty. When they refuse to dance, when my gift is denied, things start to become messy: I get hurt and angry, I resent the students—whom I blame for my plight—and I start treating them defensively, in ways that make the dance even less likely to happen.

But when I understand this liability as a trade-off for my strengths, something new and liberating arises within me. I no longer want to have my liability "fixed"—by learning how to dance solo, for example, when no one wants to dance with me—for to do that would be to compromise or even destroy my gift. Instead I want to learn how to respond more gracefully to students who refuse to dance, not projecting my limitation on them but embracing it as part of myself.

I will never be a good teacher for students who insist on remaining wallflowers throughout their careers—that is simply one of my many limits. But perhaps I can develop enough self-understanding to keep inviting the wallflowers onto the floor, holding open the possibility that some of them might hear the music, accept the invitation, and join me in the dance of teaching and learning.

TURNING AROUND TO DISCOVER THE WORLD

When way closes behind us, it is tempting to regard it simply as the result of some strategic error: had I been smarter or stronger, that door would not have slammed shut, so if I redouble my efforts, I may be able to batter it down. But that is a dangerous temptation. When I resist way closing rather than taking guidance from it, I may be ignoring the limitations inherent in my nature—which dishonors true self no less than ignoring the potentials I received as birthright gifts.

As Ruth taught me, there is as much guidance in way that closes behind us as there is in way that opens ahead of us. The opening may reveal our potentials while the closing may reveal our limits—two sides of the same coin, the coin called identity. In the spiritual domain, identity is coin of the realm, and we can learn much about our identity by examining either side of the coin.

As often happens on the spiritual journey, we have arrived at the heart of a paradox: each time a door closes, the rest of the world opens up. All we need to do is stop pounding on the door that just closed, turn around—which puts the door behind us—and welcome the largeness of life that now lies open to our souls. The door that closed kept us from entering a room, but what now lies before us is the rest of reality.

That paradox takes me back to Pendle Hill and the moment when Ruth taught me the meaning of "way closing." As I sat there fretting about the doors that had slammed in my face, I was sitting in the very place where my world would soon open wide.

Had I been able to see my own future at that moment, I would have laughed even harder than I did when Ruth's words exposed my inner mess. My future had already arrived, and its name was Pendle Hill—the place where my yearlong sabbatical stretched on for a decade, where I deepened my experiment with alternative education and started learning a new way to teach, where my struggle to understand myself and the world drew me into the writing that has become so central to my vocation.

My anxiety about way not opening, the anxiety that kept me pounding on closed doors, almost prevented me from seeing the secret hidden in plain sight: I was already standing on the ground of my new life, ready to take the next step on my journey, if only I would turn around and see the landscape that lay before me.

If we are to live our lives fully and well, we must learn to embrace the opposites, to live in a creative tension between our limits and our potentials. We must honor our limitations in ways that do not distort our nature, and we must trust and use our gifts in ways that fulfill the potentials God gave us. We must take the no of the way that closes and find the guidance it has to offer—and take the yes of the way that opens and respond with the yes of our lives.

ℭ CHAPTER IV

All the Way Down

A PERSONAL PREFACE

> Midway on our life's journey, I found myself
>> In dark woods, the right road lost. To tell
>> About those woods is hard—so tangled and rough
>
> And savage that thinking of it now, I feel
>> The old fear stirring: death is hardly more bitter.
>> And yet, to treat the good I found there as well
>
> I'll tell what I saw. . . .
>> —From THE INFERNO OF DANTE, Robert Pinsky, trans.[1]

Midway in my life's journey, "way closed" again, this time with a ferocity that felt fatal: I found myself in the dark woods called clinical depression, a total eclipse of light and hope. But after I emerged from my sojourn in the dark and had given myself several years to absorb its meaning, I saw how pivotal that passage had been on my pilgrimage toward self-hood and vocation. Though I recommend it to no one—and I do not need to, for it arrives unbidden in too many lives—depression compelled me to find the river of life hidden beneath the ice.

Still, I was unable to write about my depression for a very long time; what I learned and how I learned it remained raw to the touch. Then I was invited to contribute to a journal on the theme of the "wounded healer" in memory of Henri Nouwen, who was my mentor and my friend. If I were to honor Henri's life in a manner true to his spirit, I had no choice but to write about my own deepest wound.

Henri himself spent time on the dark side of the moon, and he talked and wrote openly about it.[2] But during the years when he and I saw a great deal of each other, I rarely spoke to him about my own darkness; even in his gracious presence, I felt too ashamed. I am no longer ashamed, but I still find depression difficult to speak about because the experience is so unspeakable. Yet Henri's spirit continues to call me and many others to more openness and vulnerability, more shared humanity and mutual healing, even—and perhaps especially—when the subject is so difficult that words seem to fail.

My only real fear about publishing these reflections is that someone may take the wrong counsel from them. Depression comes in many forms. Some are primarily genetic or biochemical and will respond only to drugs; some are primarily situational and will respond only to inner work that leads to self-knowledge, choices, and change; some lie in between.

Though I needed medication for brief periods to stabilize my brain chemistry, my depression was largely situational. I will tell the truth about it as far as I am able. But what is true for me is not necessarily true for others. I am not writing a prescription—I am simply telling my story. If it illumines your story, or the story of someone you care about, I will be grateful. If it helps you or someone you care about turn suffering into guidance for vocation, I will be more grateful still.

THE MYSTERY OF DEPRESSION

Twice in my forties I spent endless months in the snake pit of the soul. Hour by hour, day by day, I wrestled with the desire to die, sometimes so feeble in my resistance that I "practiced" ways of doing myself in. I could feel nothing except the burden of my own life and the exhaustion, the apparent futility, of trying to sustain it.

I understand why some depressed people kill themselves: they need the rest. But I do not understand why others are able to find new life in the midst of a living death, though I am one of them. I can tell you what I did to survive and, eventually, to thrive—but I cannot tell you why I was able to do those things before it was too late.

Because of my not knowing, perhaps I have learned something about the relation of depression to faith, as this story may illustrate. I once met a woman who had wrestled with depression for much of her adult life. Toward the end of a long and searching conversation, during which we talked about our shared Christian beliefs, she asked, in a voice full of misery, "Why do some people kill themselves yet others get well?"

I knew that her question came from her own struggle to stay alive, so I wanted to answer with care. But I could come up with only one response.

"I have no idea. I really have no idea."

After she left, I was haunted by regret. Couldn't I have found something more hopeful to say, even if it were not true?

A few days later, she sent me a letter saying that of all the things we had talked about, the words that stayed with her were "I have no idea." My response had given her an alternative to the cruel "Christian explanations" common in the church to which she belonged—that people who take their lives lack faith or good works or some other redeeming virtue that might move God to rescue them. My not knowing had freed her to stop judging herself for being depressed and to stop believing that God was judging her. As a result, her depression had lifted a bit.

I take two lessons from that experience. First, it is important to speak one's truth to a depressed person. Had I offered wishful thinking, it would not have touched my visitor. In depression, the built-in bunk detector that we all possess is not only turned on but is set on high.

Second, depression demands that we reject simplistic answers, both "religious" and "scientific," and learn to embrace mystery, something our culture resists. Mystery surrounds every deep experience of the human heart: the deeper we go into the heart's darkness or its light, the closer we get to the ultimate mystery of God. But our culture wants to turn mysteries into puzzles to be explained or problems to be solved, because maintaining the illusion that we can "straighten things out" makes us feel powerful. Yet mysteries never yield to solutions or fixes—and when we pretend that they do, life becomes not only more banal but also more hopeless, because the fixes never work.

Embracing the mystery of depression does not mean passivity or resignation. It means moving into a field of forces that seems alien but is in fact one's deepest self. It means waiting, watching, listening, suffering, and gathering whatever self-knowledge one can—and then making choices based on that knowledge, no matter how difficult. One begins the slow walk back to health by choosing each day things that enliven one's selfhood and resisting things that do not.

The knowledge I am talking about is not intellectual and analytical but integrative and of the heart, and the choices that lead to wholeness are not pragmatic and calculated, intended to achieve some goal, but simply and profoundly expressive of personal truth. It is a demanding path, for which no school prepares us. I know: I had to walk that path a second time because what I learned about myself the first time frightened me. I rejected my own knowing and refused to make the choices it required, and the price was a second sojourn in hell.

FROM THE OUTSIDE LOOKING IN

It is odd that some of my most vivid memories of depression involve the people who came to look in on me, since in the middle of the experience I was barely able to notice who was or was not there. Depression is the ultimate state of disconnection—it deprives one of the relatedness that is the lifeline of every living being.

I do not like to speak ungratefully of my visitors. They all meant well, and they were among the few who did not avoid me altogether. But despite their good intentions, most of them acted like Job's comforters—the friends who came to Job in his misery and offered "sympathy" that led him deeper into despair.

Some visitors, in an effort to cheer me up, would say, "It's a beautiful day. Why don't you go out and soak up some sunshine and look at the flowers? Surely that'll make you feel better."

But that advice only made me more depressed. Intellectually, I knew that the day was beautiful, but I was unable to experience that beauty through my senses, to feel it in my body. Depression is the ultimate state of disconnection, not just between people but between one's mind and one's feelings. To be reminded of that disconnection only deepened my despair.

Other people came to me and said, "But you're such a good person, Parker. You teach and write so well, and you've helped so many people. Try to remember all the good you've done, and surely you'll feel better."

That advice, too, left me more depressed, for it plunged me into the immense gap between my "good" persona and the "bad" person I then believed myself to be. When I heard those words, I thought, "One more person has been defrauded, has seen my image rather than my reality—and if people ever saw the real me, they would reject me in a flash." Depression is the ultimate state of disconnection, not only between people, and between mind and heart, but between one's self-image and public mask.

Then there were the visitors who began by saying, "I know exactly how you feel. . . ." Whatever comfort or counsel these people may have intended to speak, I heard nothing beyond their opening words, because I knew they were peddling a falsehood: no one can fully experience another person's mystery. Paradoxically, it was my friends' empathetic attempt to identify with me that made me feel even more isolated, because it was overidentification. Disconnection may be hell, but it is better than false connections.

Having not only been "comforted" by friends but having tried to comfort others in the same way, I think I understand what the syndrome is about: avoidance and denial. One of the hardest things we must do sometimes is to be present to another person's pain without trying to "fix" it, to simply stand respectfully at the edge of that person's mystery and misery. Standing there, we feel useless and powerless, which is exactly how a depressed person feels—and our unconscious need as Job's comforters is to reassure ourselves that we are not like the sad soul before us.

In an effort to avoid those feelings, I give advice, which sets me, not you, free. If you take my advice, you may get well—and if you don't get well, I did the best I could. If you fail to take my advice, there is nothing more I can do. Either way, I get relief by distancing myself from you, guilt free.

Blessedly, there were several people, family and friends, who had the courage to stand with me in a simple and healing way. One of them was a friend named Bill who, having asked my permission to do so, stopped by my home every afternoon, sat me down in a chair, knelt in front of me, removed my shoes and socks, and for half an hour simply massaged my feet. He found the one place in my body where I could still experience feeling—and feel somewhat reconnected with the human race.

Bill rarely spoke a word. When he did, he never gave advice but simply mirrored my condition. He would say, "I can sense your struggle today," or, "It feels like you are getting stronger." I could not always respond, but his words were deeply helpful: they reassured me that I could still be seen by *someone*—life-giving knowledge in the midst of an experience that makes one feel annihilated and invisible. It is impossible to put into words what my friend's ministry meant to me. Perhaps it is enough to say that I now have deep appreciation for the biblical stories of Jesus and the washing of feet.[3]

The poet Rainer Maria Rilke says, "love ... consists in this, that two solitudes protect and border and salute each other."[4] That is the kind of love my friend Bill offered. He never tried to invade my awful inwardness with false comfort or advice; he simply stood on its boundaries, modeling the respect for me and my journey—and the courage to let it be— that I myself needed if I were to endure.

This kind of love does not reflect the "functional atheism" we sometimes practice—saying pious words about God's presence in our lives but believing, on the contrary, that nothing good is going to happen unless we make it happen. Rilke describes a kind of love that neither avoids nor invades the soul's suffering. It is a love in which we represent God's love to a suffering person, a God who does not "fix" us but gives us strength by suffering with us. By standing respectfully and faithfully at the borders of another's solitude, we may mediate the love of God to a person who needs something deeper than any human being can give.

Amazingly, I was offered an unmediated sign of that love when in the middle of one sleepless night during my first depression, I heard a voice say, simply and clearly, "I love you, Parker." The words did not come audibly from without but silently from within, and they could not have come from my ego, which was too consumed by self-hatred and despair to utter them.

It was a moment of inexplicable grace — but so deep is the devastation of depression that I dismissed it. And yet that moment made its mark: I realized that my rejection of such a remarkable gift was a measure of how badly I needed help.

FROM THE INSIDE LOOKING OUT

Acknowledging my need for professional help was not easy. I had believed that going into therapy was a sign of weakness and that weakness was bad. But once I got past that barrier, I ran into another one: since *professional* has come to mean a person with a bagful of techniques and fixes, it is not always easy to find a professional who fulfills the original meaning of the word — a person grounded in a profession of faith, faith in the nature of ultimate reality, in the matrix of mercy in which our lives are embedded.

I had abortive meetings with two psychiatrists whose reliance on drugs and whose dismissive attitude toward the inner life would have made me angry enough to get well simply to spite them had I not been terminally depressed! But finally, blessedly, I found a counselor who understood what was happening to me as I needed to understand it—as a spiritual journey.

Of course, it was not the sort of spiritual journey I had hoped some day to take, not an upward climb into rarefied realms of light, not a mountaintop experience of God's presence. In fact, mine was a journey in the opposite direction: to an inner circle of hell and a face-to-face encounter with the monsters who live there.

After hours of careful listening, my therapist offered an image that helped me eventually reclaim my life. "You seem to look upon depression as the hand of an enemy trying to crush you," he said. "Do you think you could see it instead as the hand of a friend, pressing you down to ground on which it is safe to stand?"

Amid the assaults I was suffering, the suggestion that depression was my friend seemed impossibly romantic, even insulting. But something in me knew that down, down to the ground, was the direction of wholeness, thus allowing that image to begin its slow work of healing in me.

I started to understand that I had been living an ungrounded life, living at an altitude that was inherently unsafe. The problem with living at high altitude is simple: when we slip, as we always do, we have a long, long way to fall, and the landing may well kill us. The grace of being pressed down to the ground is also simple: when we slip and fall, it is usually not fatal, and we can get back up.

The altitude at which I was living had been achieved by at least four means. First, I had been trained as an intellectual not only to think—an activity I greatly value—but also to live largely in my head, the place in the human body farthest from the ground. Second, I had embraced a form of Christian faith devoted less to the experience of God than to abstractions about God, a fact that now baffles me: how did so many disembodied concepts emerge from a tradition whose central commitment is to "the Word become flesh"?

Third, my altitude had been achieved by my ego, an inflated ego that led me to think more of myself than was warranted in order to mask my fear that I was less than I should have been. Finally, it had been achieved by my ethic, a distorted ethic that led me to live by images of who I ought to be or what I ought to do, rather than by insight into my own reality, into what was true and possible and life-giving for me.

For a long time, the "oughts" had been the driving force in my life—and when I failed to live "up" to those oughts, I saw myself as a weak and faithless person. I never stopped to ask, "How does such-and-such fit my God-given nature?" or "Is such-and-such truly my gift and call?" As a result, important parts of the life I was living were not mine to live and thus were doomed to fail.

Depression was, indeed, the hand of a friend trying to press me down to ground on which it was safe to stand—the ground of my own truth, my own nature, with its complex mix of limits and gifts, liabilities and assets, darkness and light.

Eventually, I developed my own image of the "befriending" impulse behind my depression. Imagine that from early in my life, a friendly figure, standing a block away, was trying to get my attention by shouting my name, wanting to teach me some hard but healing truths about myself. But I—fearful of what I might hear or arrogantly trying to live without help or simply too busy with my ideas and ego and ethics to bother—ignored the shouts and walked away.

So this figure, still with friendly intent, came closer and shouted more loudly, but I kept walking. Ever closer it came, close enough to tap me on the shoulder, but I walked on. Frustrated by my unresponsiveness, the figure threw stones at my back, then struck me with a stick, still wanting simply to get my attention. But despite the pain, I kept walking away.

Over the years, the befriending intent of this figure never disappeared but became obscured by the frustration caused by my refusal to turn around. Since shouts and taps, stones and sticks had failed to do the trick, there was only one thing left: drop the nuclear bomb called depression on me, not with the intent to kill but as a last-ditch effort to get me to turn and ask the simple question, "What do you want?" When I was finally able to make that turn—and start to absorb and act on the self-knowledge that then became available to me—I began to get well.

The figure calling to me all those years was, I believe, what Thomas Merton calls "true self." This is not the ego self that wants to inflate us (or deflate us, another form of self-distortion), not the intellectual self that wants to hover above the mess of life in clear but ungrounded ideas, not the ethical self that wants to live by some abstract moral code. It is the self planted in us by the God who made us in God's own image — the self that wants nothing more, or less, than for us to be who we were created to be.

True self is true friend. One ignores or rejects such friendship only at one's peril.

THE WAY TO GOD IS DOWN

When I was finally able to turn around and ask, "What do you want?" the answer was clear: I want you to embrace this descent into hell as a journey toward selfhood — and a journey toward God.

I had always imagined God to be in the same general direction as everything else that I valued: up. I had failed to appreciate the meaning of some words that had intrigued me since I first heard them in seminary — Tillich's description of God as the "ground of being." I had to be forced underground before I could understand that the way to God is not up but down.

The underground is a dangerous but potentially life-giving place to which depression takes us; a place where we come to understand that the self is not set apart or special or superior but is a common mix of good and evil, darkness and light; a place where we can finally embrace the humanity we share with others. That is the best image I can offer not only of the underground but also of the field of forces surrounding the experience of God.

Years ago, someone told me that humility is central to the spiritual life. That made sense to me: I was proud to think of myself as humble! But this person did not tell me that the path to humility, for some of us at least, goes through humiliation, where we are brought low, rendered powerless, stripped of pretenses and defenses, and left feeling fraudulent, empty, and useless—a humiliation that allows us to regrow our lives from the ground up, from the humus of common ground.

The spiritual journey is full of paradoxes. One of them is that the humiliation that brings us down—down to ground on which it is safe to stand and to fall—eventually takes us to a firmer and fuller sense of self. When people ask me how it felt to emerge from depression, I can give only one answer: I felt at home in my own skin, and at home on the face of the earth, for the first time.

Florida Scott Maxwell put it in terms more elegant than mine: "You need only claim the events of your life to make yourself yours. When you truly possess all you have been and done . . . you are fierce with reality."[5] I now know myself to be a person of weakness and strength, liability and giftedness, darkness and light. I now know that to be whole means to reject none of it but to embrace all of it.

Some may say that this embrace is narcissistic, an obsession with self at the expense of others, but that is not how I experience it. When I ignored my own truth on behalf of a distorted ego and ethic, I led a false life that caused others pain—for which I can only ask forgiveness. When I started attending to my own truth, more of that truth became available in my work and my relationships. I now know that anything one can do on behalf of true self is done ultimately in the service of others.

Others may say that "embracing one's wholeness" is just fancy talk for permission to sin, but again my experience is to the contrary. To embrace weakness, liability, and darkness as part of who I am gives that part less sway over me, because all it ever wanted was to be acknowledged as part of my whole self.

At the same time, embracing one's wholeness makes life more demanding—because once you do that, you must live your whole life. One of the most painful discoveries I made in the midst of the dark woods of depression was that a part of me wanted to stay depressed. As long as I clung to this living death, life became easier; little was expected of me, certainly not serving others.

I had missed the deep meaning of a biblical teaching that I had always regarded as a no-brainer: "I set before you life or death, blessing or curse. Therefore, choose life" (Deuteronomy 30:19). Why, I wondered, would God waste precious breath on saying something so obvious? I had failed to understand the perverse comfort we sometimes get from choosing death in life, exempting ourselves from the challenge of using our gifts, of living our lives in authentic relationship with others.

I was finally able to say yes to life, a choice for which I am grateful beyond measure, though how I found that yes remains a mystery to me. At one fork in the long road back to wholeness—when I was in fact walking along a country road past a freshly plowed field—I found a poem taking form within me. I offer it, along with my unknowing, as a token of hope to anyone who may be enduring the harrowing of depression.

HARROWING

The plow has savaged this sweet field
Misshapen clods of earth kicked up
Rocks and twisted roots exposed to view
Last year's growth demolished by the blade.
I have plowed my life this way
Turned over a whole history
Looking for the roots of what went wrong
Until my face is ravaged, furrowed, scarred.

Enough. The job is done.
Whatever's been uprooted, let it be
Seedbed for the growing that's to come.
I plowed to unearth last year's reasons—

The farmer plows to plant a greening season.

CHAPTER V

Leading from Within

BACK TO THE WORLD

From the depths of depression, I turn now to our shared vocation of leadership in the world of action. This may seem more like a leap than a turn, but none of the great wisdom traditions would look upon this segue with surprise. Go far enough on the inner journey, they all tell us—go past ego toward true self—and you end up not lost in narcissism but returning to the world, bearing more gracefully the responsibilities that come with being human.

Those words are more than a device to weave these chapters together—they are a faithful reflection of what happened to me once I passed through the valley of depression. At the end of that descent into darkness and isolation, I found myself reengaged with community, better able to offer leadership to the causes I care about.

"Leadership" is a concept we often resist. It seems immodest, even self-aggrandizing, to think of ourselves as leaders. But if it is true that we are made for community, then leadership is everyone's vocation, and it can be an evasion to insist that it is not. When we live in the close-knit ecosystem called community, everyone follows and everyone leads.

Even I—a person who is unfit to be president of anything, who once galloped away from institutions on a high horse— have come to understand that for better or for worse, I lead by word and deed *simply because I am here doing what I do.* If you are also here, doing what you do, then you also exercise leadership of some sort.

But modesty is only one reason we resist the idea of leadership; cynicism about our most visible leaders is another. In America, at least, our declining public life has bred too many self-serving leaders who seem lacking in ethics, compassion, and vision. But if we look again at the headlines, we will find leaders worthy of respect in places we often ignore: in South Africa, Latin America, and eastern Europe, for example, places where people who have known great darkness have emerged to lead others toward the light.

The words of one of those people—Václav Havel, playwright, dissident, prisoner, and now president of the Czech Republic—take us to the heart of what leadership means in settings both large and small. In 1990, a few months after Czechoslovakia freed itself from communist rule, Havel addressed a joint session of the U.S. Congress: "The communist type of totalitarian system has left both our nations, Czechs and Slovaks, . . . a legacy of countless dead, an infinite spectrum of human suffering, profound economic decline, and, above all, enormous human humiliation. It has brought us horrors that fortunately you have never known. . . ." (I think we Americans should confess that some in our country *have* known such horrors.)

> It has [also] given us something positive: a special capacity to look, from time to time, somewhat further than those who have not undergone this bitter experience. Someone who cannot move and live a normal life because he is pinned under a boulder has more time to think about his hopes than someone who is not trapped in this way.

> What I am trying to say is this: we must all learn many things from you, from how to educate our offspring and how to elect our representatives to how to organize our economic life so that it will lead to prosperity and not poverty. But this doesn't have to be merely assistance from the well-educated, the powerful, and the wealthy to those who have nothing to offer in return.

> We too can offer something to you: our experience and the knowledge that has come from it. . . . The specific experience I'm talking about has given me one certainty: Consciousness precedes Being, and not the other way around, as Marxists claim. For this reason, the salvation of this human world lies nowhere else than in the human heart, in the human power

to reflect, in human modesty, and in human responsibility. Without a global revolution in the sphere of human consciousness, nothing will change for the better . . . and the catastrophe toward which this world is headed, whether it be it ecological, social, demographic or a general breakdown of civilization, will be unavoidable.[1]

The power for authentic leadership, Havel tells us, is found not in external arrangements but in the human heart. Authentic leaders in every setting—from families to nation-states—aim at liberating the heart, their own and others', so that its powers can liberate the world.

I cannot imagine a stronger affirmation from a more credible source of the significance of the inner life in the external affairs of our time: "Consciousness precedes Being" and "the salvation of this human world lies nowhere else than in the human heart." Material reality, Havel claims, is not the fundamental factor in the movement of human history. Consciousness is. Awareness is. Thought is. Spirit is. These are not the ephemera of dreams. They are the inner Archimedean points from which oppressed people have gained the leverage to lift immense boulders and release transformative change.

But there is another truth that Havel, a guest in our country, was too polite to tell. It is not only the Marxists who have believed that matter is more powerful than consciousness, that economics is more fundamental than spirit, that the flow of cash creates more reality than the flow of visions and ideas.

Capitalists have believed these things too—and though Havel was too polite to say this to us, honesty obliges us to say it to ourselves.

We capitalists have a long and crippling legacy of believing in the power of external realities much more deeply than we believe in the power of the inner life. How many times have you heard or said, "Those are inspiring notions, but the hard reality is . . ."? How many times have you worked in systems based on the belief that the only changes that matter are the ones you can measure or count? How many times have you watched people kill off creativity by treating traditional policies and practices as absolute constraints on what we can do?

This is not just a Marxist problem; it is a human problem. But the great insight of our spiritual traditions is that we— especially those of us who enjoy political freedom and relative affluence—are not victims of that society: we are its co-creators. We live in and through a complex interaction of spirit and matter, of the powers inside of us and the stuff "out there" in the world. External reality does not impinge upon us as an ultimate constraint: if we who are privileged find ourselves confined, it is only because we have conspired in our own imprisonment.

The spiritual traditions do not deny the reality of the outer world. They simply claim that we help make that world by projecting our spirit on it, for better or for worse. If our institutions are rigid, it is because our hearts fear change; if they set us in mindless competition with each other, it is because we value victory over all else; if they are heedless of human well-being, it is because something in us is heartless as well.

We can make choices about what we are going to project, and with those choices we help grow the world that is. Consciousness precedes being: consciousness, yours and mine, can form, deform, or reform our world. Our complicity in world making is a source of awesome and sometimes painful responsibility—and a source of profound hope for change. It is the ground of our common call to leadership, the truth that makes leaders of us all.

SHADOWS AND SPIRITUALITY

A leader is someone with the power to project either shadow or light onto some part of the world and onto the lives of the people who dwell there. A leader shapes the ethos in which others must live, an ethos as light-filled as heaven or as shadowy as hell. A *good* leader is intensely aware of the interplay of inner shadow and light, lest the act of leadership do more harm than good.

I think, for example, of teachers who create the conditions under which young people must spend so many hours: some shine a light that allows new growth to flourish, while others cast a shadow under which seedlings die. I think of parents who generate similar effects in the lives of their families or of clergy who do the same to entire congregations. I think of corporate CEOs whose daily decisions are driven by inner dynamics but who rarely reflect on those motives or even believe they are real.

We have a long tradition of approaching leadership via the "power of positive thinking." I want to counterbalance that approach by paying special attention to the tendency we have as leaders to project more shadow than light. Leadership is hard work for which one is regularly criticized and rarely rewarded, so it is understandable that we need to bolster ourselves with positive thoughts. But by failing to look at our shadows, we feed a dangerous delusion that leaders too often indulge: that our efforts are always well intended, our power is always benign, and the problem is always in those difficult people whom we are trying to lead!

Those of us who readily embrace leadership, especially public leadership, tend toward extroversion, which often means ignoring what is happening inside ourselves. If we have any sort of inner life, we "compartmentalize" it, walling it off from our public work. This, of course, allows the shadow to grow unchecked until it emerges, larger than life, in the public realm, a problem we are well acquainted with in our own domestic politics. Leaders need not only the technical skills to manage the external world but also the spiritual skills to journey inward toward the source of both shadow and light.

Spirituality, like leadership, is a hard thing to define. But Annie Dillard has given us a vivid image of what authentic spirituality is about: "In the deeps are the violence and terror of which psychology has warned us. But if you ride these monsters down, if you drop with them farther over the world's rim, you find what our sciences cannot locate or name, the substrate, the ocean or matrix or ether which buoys the rest, which gives goodness its power for good, and evil its power for evil, the unified field: our complex and inexplicable caring for each other, and for our life together here. This is given. It is not learned."[2]

Here Dillard names two crucial features of any spiritual journey. One is that it will take us inward and downward, toward the hardest realities of our lives, rather than outward and upward toward abstraction, idealization, and exhortation. The spiritual journey runs counter to the power of positive thinking.

Why must we go in and down? Because as we do so, we will meet the darkness that we carry within ourselves—the ultimate source of the shadows that we project onto other people. If we do not understand that the enemy is within, we will find a thousand ways of making someone "out there" into the enemy, becoming leaders who oppress rather than liberate others.

But, says Annie Dillard, if we ride those monsters all the way down, we break through to something precious—to "the unified field, our complex and inexplicable caring for each other," to the community we share beneath the broken surface of our lives. Good leadership comes from people who have penetrated their own inner darkness and arrived at the place where we are at one with one another, people who can lead the rest of us to a place of "hidden wholeness" because they have been there and know the way.

Václav Havel would be familiar with the journey Annie Dillard describes, because downward is where you go when you spend years "pinned under a boulder." That image suggests not only the political oppression under which all Czechs were forced to live but also the psychological depression Havel fell into as he struggled to survive under the communist regime.

In 1975, that depression compelled Havel to write an open letter of protest to Gustav Husak, head of the Czecho-slovakian Communist party. His letter—which got Havel thrown in jail and became the text of an underground move-ment that fomented the "Velvet Revolution" of 1989—was, in Havel's own words, an act of "autotherapy," an alternative to suicide, his expression of the decision to live divided no more. As Vincent and Jane Kavaloski have written, Havel "felt that he could remain silent only at the risk of 'living a lie,' and destroying himself from within."[3]

That is the choice before us when we are "pinned under a boulder" of any sort, the same choice Nelson Mandela made by using twenty-eight years in prison to prepare inwardly for leadership instead of drowning in despair. Under the most oppressive circumstances, people like Mandela, Havel, and uncounted others go all the way down, travel through their inner darkness—and emerge with the capacity to lead the rest of us toward community, toward "our complex and inexplicable caring for each other."

Annie Dillard offers a powerful image of the inner journey and tells us what might happen if we were to take it. But why would anybody want to take a journey of that sort, with its multiple difficulties and dangers? Everything in us cries out against it—which is why we externalize everything. It is so much easier to deal with the external world, to spend our lives manipulating material and institutions and other people instead of dealing with our own souls. We like to talk about the outer world as if it were infinitely complex and demanding, but it is a cakewalk compared to the labyrinth of our inner lives!

Here is a small story from my life about why one might want to take the inner journey. In my early forties, I decided to go on the program called Outward Bound. I was on the edge of my first depression, a fact I knew only dimly at the time, and I thought Outward Bound might be a place to shake up my life and learn some things I needed to know.

I chose the weeklong course at Hurricane Island, off the coast of Maine. I should have known from that name what was in store for me; next time I will sign up for the course at Happy Gardens or Pleasant Valley! Though it was a week of great teaching, deep community, and genuine growth, it was also a week of fear and loathing.

In the middle of that week, I faced the challenge I feared most. One of our instructors backed me up to the edge of a cliff 110 feet above solid ground. He tied a very thin rope to my waist—a rope that looked ill-kempt to me and seemed to be starting to unravel—and told me to start "rappelling" down that cliff.

"Do what?" I said.

"Just go!" the instructor explained, in typical Outward Bound fashion.

So I went—and immediately slammed into a ledge, some four feet down from the edge of the cliff, with bone-jarring, brain-jarring force.

The instructor looked down at me: "I don't think you've quite got it."

"Right," said I, being in no position to disagree. "So what am I supposed to do?"

"The only way to do this," he said, "is to lean back as far as you can. You have to get your body at right angles to the cliff so that your weight will be on your feet. It's counterintuitive, but it's the only way that works."

I knew that he was wrong, of course. I knew that the trick was to hug the mountain, to stay as close to the rock face as I could. So I tried it again, my way—and slammed into the next ledge, another four feet down.

"You still don't have it," the instructor said helpfully.

"OK," I said, "tell me again what I am supposed to do."

"Lean way back," said he, "and take the next step."

The next step was a very big one, but I took it—and, wonder of wonders, it worked. I leaned back into empty space, eyes fixed on the heavens in prayer, made tiny, tiny moves with my feet, and started descending down the rock face, gaining confidence with every step.

I was about halfway down when the second instructor called up from below: "Parker, I think you'd better stop and see what's just below your feet." I lowered my eyes very slowly—so as not to shift my weight—and saw that I was approaching a deep hole in the face of the rock.

To get down, I would have to get around that hole, which meant I could not maintain the straight line of descent I had started to get comfortable with. I would need to change course and swing myself around that hole, to the left or to the right. I knew for a certainty that attempting to do so would lead directly to my death—so I froze, paralyzed with fear.

The second instructor let me hang there, trembling, in silence, for what seemed like a very long time. Finally, she shouted up these helpful words: "Parker, is anything wrong?"

To this day, I do not know where my words came from, though I have twelve witnesses to the fact that I spoke them. In a high, squeaky voice, I said, "I don't want to talk about it."

"Then," said the second instructor, "it's time that you learned the Outward Bound motto."

"Oh, keen," I thought. "I'm about to die, and she's going to give me a motto!"

But then she shouted ten words I hope never to forget, words whose impact and meaning I can still feel: "If you can't get out of it, get into it!"

I had long believed in the concept of "the word become flesh," but until that moment, I had not experienced it. My teacher spoke words so compelling that they bypassed my mind, went into my flesh, and animated my legs and feet. No helicopter would come to rescue me; the instructor on the cliff would not pull me up with the rope; there was no parachute in my backpack to float me to the ground. There was no way out of my dilemma except to get into it—so my feet started to move, and in a few minutes I made it safely down.

Why would anyone want to embark on the daunting inner journey about which Annie Dillard writes? Because there is no way out of one's inner life, so one had better get into it. On the inward and downward spiritual journey, the only way out is in and through.

OUT OF THE SHADOW AND INTO THE LIGHT

If we, as leaders, are to cast less shadow and more light, we need to ride certain monsters all the way down, explore the shadows they create, and experience the transformation that can come as we "get into" our own spiritual lives. Here is a bestiary of five such monsters. The five are not theoretical for me; I became personally acquainted with each of them during my descent into depression. They are also the monsters I work with when I lead retreats where leaders of many sorts—CEOs, clergy, parents, teachers, citizens, and seekers—take an inward journey toward common ground.

The first shadow-casting monster is insecurity about identity and worth. Many leaders have an extroverted personality that makes this shadow hard to see. But extroversion sometimes develops as a way to cope with self-doubt: we plunge into external activity to prove that we are worthy—or simply to evade the question. There is a well-known form of this syndrome, especially among men, in which our identity becomes so dependent on performing some external role that we become depressed, and even die, when that role is taken away.

When we are insecure about our own identities, we create settings that deprive other people of *their* identities as a way of buttressing our own. This happens all the time in families, where parents who do not like themselves give their children low self-esteem. It happens at work as well: how often I phone a business or professional office and hear, "Dr. Jones's office—this is Nancy speaking." The boss has a title and a last name but the person (usually a woman) who answers the phone has neither, because the boss has decreed that it will be that way.

There are dynamics in all kinds of institutions that deprive the many of their identity so the few can enhance their own, as if identity were a zero-sum game, a win-lose situation. Look into a classroom, for example, where an insecure teacher is forcing students to be passive stenographers of the teacher's store of knowledge, leaving the teacher with more sense of selfhood and the vulnerable students with less. Or look in on a hospital where the doctors turn patients into objects—"the kidney in Room 410"—as a way of claiming superiority at the very time when vulnerable patients desperately need a sense of self.

Things are not always this way, of course. There are settings and institutions led by people whose identities do not depend on depriving others of theirs. If you are in that kind of family or office or school or hospital, your sense of self is enhanced by leaders who know who they are.

These leaders possess a gift available to all who take an inner journey: the knowledge that identity does not depend on the role we play or the power it gives us over others. It depends only on the simple fact that we are children of God, valued in and for ourselves. When a leader is grounded in that knowledge, what happens in the family, the office, the classroom, the hospital can be life-giving for all concerned.

A second shadow inside many of us is the belief that the universe is a battleground, hostile to human interests. Notice how often we use images of warfare as we go about our work, especially in organizations. We talk about tactics and strategies, allies and enemies, wins and losses, "do or die." If we fail to be fiercely competitive, the imagery suggests, we will surely lose, because the world we live in is essentially a vast combat zone.

Unfortunately, life is full of self-fulfilling prophecies. The tragedy of this inner shadow, our fear of losing a fight, is that it helps create conditions where people feel compelled to live as if they were at war. Yes, the world is competitive, but largely because we make it so. Some of our best institutions, from corporations to change agencies to schools, are learning that there is another way of doing business, a way that is consensual, cooperative, communal: they are fulfilling a different prophecy and creating a different reality.

The gift we receive on the inner journey is the insight that the universe is working together for good. The structure of reality is not the structure of a battle. Reality is not out to get anybody. Yes, there is death, but it is part of the cycle of life, and when we learn to move gracefully with that cycle, a great harmony comes into our lives. The spiritual truth that harmony is more fundamental than warfare in the nature of reality itself could transform this leadership shadow—and transform our institutions as well.

A third shadow common among leaders is "functional atheism," the belief that ultimate responsibility for everything rests with us. This is the unconscious, unexamined conviction that if anything decent is going to happen here, we are the ones who must make it happen—a conviction held even by people who talk a good game about God.

This shadow causes pathology on every level of our lives. It leads us to impose our will on others, stressing our relationships, sometimes to the point of breaking. It often eventuates in burnout, depression, and despair, as we learn that the world will not bend to our will and we become embittered about that fact. Functional atheism is the shadow that drives collective frenzy as well. It explains why the average group can tolerate no more than fifteen seconds of silence: if we are not making noise, we believe, nothing good is happening and something must be dying.

The gift we receive on the inner journey is the knowledge that ours is not the only act in town. Not only are there other acts out there, but some of them are even better than ours, at least occasionally! We learn that we need not carry the whole load but can share it with others, liberating us and empowering them. We learn that sometimes we are free to lay the load down altogether. The great community asks us to do only what we are able and trust the rest to other hands.

A fourth shadow within and among us is fear, especially our fear of the natural chaos of life. Many of us—parents and teachers and CEOs—are deeply devoted to eliminating all remnants of chaos from the world. We want to organize and orchestrate things so thoroughly that messiness will never bubble up around us and threaten to overwhelm us (for "messiness" read dissent, innovation, challenge, and change). In families and churches and corporations, this shadow is projected as rigidity of rules and procedures, creating an ethos that is imprisoning rather than empowering. (Then, of course, the mess we must deal with is the prisoners trying to break out!)

The insight we receive on the inner journey is that chaos is the precondition to creativity: as every creation myth has it, life itself emerged from the void. Even what has been created needs to be returned to chaos from time to time so that it can be regenerated in more vital form. When a leader fears chaos so deeply as to try to eliminate it, the shadow of death will fall across everything that leader approaches—for the ultimate answer to all of life's messiness is death.

My final example of the shadows that leaders project is, paradoxically, the denial of death itself. Though we sometimes kill things off well before their time, we also live in denial of the fact that all things must die in due course. Leaders who participate in this denial often demand that the people around them keep resuscitating things that are no longer alive. Projects and programs that should have been unplugged long ago are kept on life support to accommodate the insecurities of a leader who does not want anything to die on his or her watch.

Within our denial of death lurks fear of another sort: the fear of failure. In most organizations, failure means a pink slip in your box, even if that failure, that "little death," was suffered in the service of high purpose. It is interesting that science, so honored in our culture, seems to have transcended this particular fear. A good scientist does not fear the death of a hypothesis, because that "failure" clarifies the steps that need to be taken toward truth, sometimes more than a hypothesis that succeeds. The best leaders in every setting reward people for taking worthwhile risks even if they are likely to fail. These leaders know that the death of an initiative—if it was tested for good reasons—is always a source of new learning.

The gift we receive on the inner journey is the knowledge that death finally comes to everything—and yet death does not have the final word. By allowing something to die when its time is due, we create the conditions under which new life can emerge.

INNER WORK IN COMMUNITY

Can we help each other deal with the inner issues inherent in leadership? We can, and I believe we must. Our frequent failure as leaders to deal with our inner lives leaves too many individuals and institutions in the dark. From the family to the corporation to the body politic, we are in trouble partly because of the shadows I have named. Since we can't get out of it, we must get into it—by helping each other explore our inner lives. What might that help look like?

First, we could lift up the value of "inner work." That phrase should become commonplace in families, schools, and religious institutions, at least, helping us understand that inner work is as real as outer work and involves skills one can develop, skills like journaling, reflective reading, spiritual friendship, meditation, and prayer. We can teach our children something that their parents did not always know: if people skimp on their inner work, their outer work will suffer as well.

Second, we could spread the word that inner work, though it is a deeply *personal* matter, is not necessarily a *private* matter: inner work can be helped along in community. Indeed, doing inner work together is a vital counterpoint to doing it alone. Left to our own devices, we may delude ourselves in ways that others can help us correct.

But *how* a community offers such help is a critical question. We are surrounded by communities based on the practice of "setting each other straight"—an ultimately totalitarian practice bound to drive the shy soul into hiding. Fortunately, there are other models of corporate discernment and support.

For example, there is the Quaker clearness committee mentioned earlier in this book. You take a personal issue to this small group of people who are prohibited from suggesting "fixes" or giving you advice but who for three hours pose honest, open questions to help you discover your inner truth. Communal processes of this sort are supportive but not invasive. They help us probe questions and possibilities but forbid us from rendering judgment, allowing us to serve as midwives to a birth of consciousness that can only come from within.[4]

The key to this form of community involves holding a paradox—the paradox of having relationships in which we protect each other's aloneness. We must come together in ways that respect the solitude of the soul, that avoid the unconscious violence we do when we try to save each other, that evoke our capacity to hold another life without dishonoring its mystery, never trying to coerce the other into meeting our own needs.

It *is* possible for people to be together that way, though it may be hard to see evidence of that fact in everyday life. My evidence comes in part from my journey through clinical depression, from the healing I experienced as a few people found ways to be present to me without violating my soul's integrity. Because they were not driven by their own fears, the fears that lead us either to "fix" or abandon each other, they provided me with a lifeline to the human race. That lifeline constituted the most profound form of leadership I can imagine—leading a suffering person back to life from a living death.

Third, we can remind each other of the dominant role that fear plays in our lives, of all the ways that fear forecloses the potentials I have explored in this chapter. It is no accident that all of the world's wisdom traditions address the fact of fear, for all of them originated in the human struggle to overcome this ancient enemy. And all of these traditions, despite their great diversity, unite in one exhortation to those who walk in their ways: "Be not afraid."

As one who is no stranger to fear, I have had to read those words with care so as not to twist them into a discouraging counsel of perfection. "Be not afraid" does not mean we cannot *have* fear. Everyone has fear, and people who embrace the call to leadership often find fear abounding. Instead, the words say we do not need to *be* the fear we have. We do not have to lead from a place of fear, thereby engendering a world in which fear is multiplied.

We have places of fear inside of us, but we have other places as well—places with names like trust and hope and faith. We can choose to lead from one of *those* places, to stand on ground that is not riddled with the fault lines of fear, to move toward others from a place of promise instead of anxiety. As we stand in one of those places, fear may remain close at hand and our spirits may still tremble. But now we stand on ground that will support us, ground from which we can lead others toward a more trustworthy, more hopeful, more faithful way of being in the world.

CHAPTER VI

There Is a Season

FROM LANGUAGE TO LIFE

Throughout this book, I have looked at selfhood and vocation through metaphorical lenses, from the "seed" of true self that is planted in the world at our birth to the "journey" we take through darkness toward the light. I end with yet another metaphor, looking at selfhood and vocation through the turning of the seasons.

The seasonal metaphor deepens our understanding of the others. Seeds move through their life stages in an endless cycle of seasons—and the cycle of seasons reminds us that the journey never ends. Our lives participate in the myth of eternal return: we circle around and spiral down, never finally answering the questions "Who am I?" and "Whose am I?" but, in the words of Rilke, "living the questions" throughout our lives.[1]

The seasonal metaphor also gives our inquiry new scope. It takes the quest for selfhood and vocation out beyond its origins in the depths of the inner life, out beyond the human community and its call to leadership, into the world of nature, that most vast of all the visible worlds in which our lives are embedded.

Metaphors are more than literary devices, of course: most of us use metaphors, albeit unconsciously, to name our experience of life. But these personal metaphors do much more than describe reality as we know it. Animated by the imagination, one of the most vital powers we possess, our metaphors often *become* reality, transmuting themselves from language into the living of our lives.

I know people who say, "Life is like a game of chance—some win, some lose." But that metaphor can create a fatalism about losing or an obsession with beating the odds. I know other people who say, "Life is like a battlefield—you get the enemy, or the enemy gets you." But that metaphor can result in enemies around every corner and a constant sense of siege. We do well to choose our metaphors wisely.

Seasons is a wise metaphor for the movement of life, I think. It suggests that life is neither a battlefield nor a game of chance but something infinitely richer, more promising, more real. The notion that our lives are like the eternal cycle of the seasons does not deny the struggle or the joy, the loss or the gain, the darkness or the light, but encourages us to embrace it all—and to find in all of it opportunities for growth.

If we lived close to nature in an agricultural society, the seasons as metaphor and fact would continually frame our lives. But the master metaphor of our era does not come from agriculture—it comes from manufacturing. We do not believe that we "grow" our lives—we believe that we "make" them. Just listen to how we use the word in everyday speech: we make time, make friends, make meaning, make money, make a living, make love.

I once heard Alan Watts observe that a Chinese child will ask, "How does a baby grow?" But an American child will ask, "How do you make a baby?" From an early age, we absorb our culture's arrogant conviction that we manufacture everything, reducing the world to mere "raw material" that lacks all value until we impose our designs and labor on it.

If we accept the notion that our lives are dependent on an inexorable cycle of seasons, on a play of powers that we can conspire with but never control, we run headlong into a culture that insists, against all evidence, that we can make whatever kind of life we want, whenever we want it. Deeper still, we run headlong into our own egos, which want desperately to believe that we are always in charge.

We need to challenge and reform these distortions of culture and ego—reform them toward ways of thinking and doing and being that are rooted in respect for the living ecology of life. Unlike "raw material" on which we make all the demands, this ecology makes demands on us even as it sustains our lives. We are here not only to transform the world but also to be transformed.

Transformation is difficult, so it is good to know that there is comfort as well as challenge in the metaphor of life as a cycle of seasons. Illumined by that image, we see that we are not alone in the universe. We are participants in a vast communion of being, and if we open ourselves to its guidance, we can learn anew how to live in this great and gracious community of truth. We can, and we must—if we want our sciences to be humane, our institutions to be sustaining, our healings to be deep, our lives to be true.

AUTUMN

Autumn is a season of great beauty, but it is also a season of decline: the days grow shorter, the light is suffused, and summer's abundance decays toward winter's death. Faced with this inevitable winter, what does nature do in autumn? It scatters the seeds that will bring new growth in the spring—and scatters them with amazing abandon.

In my own experience of autumn, I am rarely aware that seeds are being planted. Instead, my mind is on the fact that the green growth of summer is browning and beginning to die. My delight in the autumn colors is always tinged with melancholy, a sense of impending loss that is only heightened by the beauty all around. I am drawn down by the prospect of death more than I am lifted by the hope of new life.

But as I explore autumn's paradox of dying and seeding, I feel the power of metaphor. In the autumnal events of my own experience, I am easily fixated on surface appearances—on the decline of meaning, the decay of relationships, the death of a work. And yet if I look more deeply, I may see the myriad possibilities being planted to bear fruit in some season yet to come.

In retrospect, I can see in my own life what I could not see at the time—how the job I lost helped me find work I needed to do, how the "road closed" sign turned me toward terrain I needed to travel, how losses that felt irredeemable forced me to discern meanings I needed to know. On the surface, it seemed that life was lessening, but silently and lavishly the seeds of new life were always being sown.

This hopeful notion that living is hidden within dying is surely enhanced by the visual glories of autumn. What artist would ever have painted a season of dying with such a vivid palette if nature had not done it first? Does death possess a beauty that we—who fear death, who find it ugly and obscene—cannot see? How shall we understand autumn's testimony that death and elegance go hand in hand?

For me, the words that come closest to answering those questions are the words of Thomas Merton: "There is in all visible things . . . a hidden wholeness."[2] In the visible world of nature, a great truth is concealed in plain sight: diminishment and beauty, darkness and light, death and life are not opposites. They are held together in the paradox of "hidden wholeness."

In a paradox, opposites do not negate each—they cohere in mysterious unity at the heart of reality. Deeper still, they need each other for health, as my body needs to breathe in as well as breathe out. But in a culture that prefers the ease of either-or thinking to the complexities of paradox, we have a hard time holding opposites together. We want light without darkness, the glories of spring and summer without the demands of autumn and winter—and the Faustian bargains we make fail to sustain our lives.

When we so fear the dark that we demand light around the clock, there can be only one result: artificial light that is glaring and graceless and, beyond its borders, a darkness that grows ever more terrifying as we try to hold it off. Split off from each other, neither darkness nor light is fit for human habitation. But if we allow the paradox of darkness and light to be, the two will conspire to bring wholeness and health to every living thing.

Autumn constantly reminds me that my daily dyings are necessary precursors to new life. If I try to "make" a life that defies the diminishments of autumn, the life I end up with will be artificial, at best, and utterly colorless as well. But when I yield to the endless interplay of living and dying, dying and living, the life I am given will be real and colorful, fruitful and whole.

WINTER

The little deaths of autumn are mild precursors to the rigor mortis of winter. The southern humorist Roy Blount has opined that in the Upper Midwest, where I live, what we get in winter is not weather but divine retribution. He believes that someone here once did something very, very bad, and we are still paying the price for that transgression!

Winter here is a demanding season—and not everyone appreciates the discipline. It is a season when death's victory can seem supreme: few creatures stir, plants do not visibly grow, and nature feels like our enemy. And yet the rigors of winter, like the diminishments of autumn, are accompanied by amazing gifts.

One gift is beauty, different from the beauty of autumn but somehow lovelier still: I am not sure that any sight or sound on earth is as exquisite as the hushed descent of a sky full of snow. Another gift is the reminder that times of dormancy and deep rest are essential to all living things. Despite all appearances, of course, nature is not dead in winter—it has gone underground to renew itself and prepare for spring. Winter is a time when we are admonished, and even inclined, to do the same for ourselves.

But for me, winter has an even greater gift to give. It comes when the sky is clear, the sun is brilliant, the trees are bare, and first snow is yet to come. It is the gift of utter clarity. In winter, one can walk into woods that had been opaque with summer growth only a few months earlier and see the trees clearly, singly and together, and see the ground they are rooted in.

A few years ago, my father died. He was more than a good man, and the months following his death were a long, hard winter for me. But in the midst of that ice and loss, I came into a certain clarity that I lacked when he was alive. I saw something that had been concealed when the luxuriance of his love surrounded me—saw how I had relied on him to help me cushion life's harsher blows. When he could no longer do that, my first thought was, "Now I must do it for myself." But as time went on, I saw a deeper truth: it never was my father absorbing those blows but a larger and deeper grace that he taught me to rely on.

When my father was alive, I confused the teaching with the teacher. My teacher is gone now, but the grace is still there—and my clarity about that fact has allowed his teaching to take deeper root in me. Winter clears the landscape, however brutally, giving us a chance to see ourselves and each other more clearly, to see the very ground of our being.

In the Upper Midwest, newcomers often receive a classic piece of wintertime advice: "The winters will drive you crazy until you learn to get out into them." Here people spend good money on warm clothing so that they can get outdoors and avoid the "cabin fever" that comes from huddling fearfully by the fire during the hard-frozen months. If you live here long, you learn that a daily walk into the winter world will fortify the spirit by taking you boldly to the very heart of the season you fear.

Our inward winters take many forms—failure, betrayal, depression, death. But every one of them, in my experience, yields to the same advice: "The winters will drive you crazy until you learn to get out into them." Until we enter boldly into the fears we most want to avoid, those fears will dominate our lives. But when we walk directly into them—protected from frostbite by the warm garb of friendship or inner discipline or spiritual guidance—we can learn what they have to teach us. Then we discover once again that the cycle of the seasons is trustworthy and life-giving, even in the most dismaying season of all.

SPRING

I will wax romantic about spring and its splendors in a moment, but first there is a hard truth to be told: before spring becomes beautiful, it is plug ugly, nothing but mud and muck. I have walked in the early spring through fields that will suck your boots off, a world so wet and woeful it makes you yearn for the return of ice. But in that muddy mess, the conditions for rebirth are being created.

I love the fact that the word *humus*—the decayed vegetable matter that feeds the roots of plants—comes from the same root that gives rise to the word *humility*. It is a blessed etymology. It helps me understand that the humiliating events of life, the events that leave "mud on my face" or that "make my name mud," may create the fertile soil in which something new can grow.

Though spring begins slowly and tentatively, it grows with a tenacity that never fails to touch me. The smallest and most tender shoots insist on having their way, coming up through ground that looked, only a few weeks earlier, as if it would never grow anything again. The crocuses and snowdrops do not bloom for long. But their mere appearance, however brief, is always a harbinger of hope, and from those small beginnings, hope grows at a geometric rate. The days get longer, the winds get warmer, and the world grows green again.

In my own life, as my winters segue into spring, I find it not only hard to cope with mud but also hard to credit the small harbingers of larger life to come, hard to hope until the outcome is secure. Spring teaches me to look more carefully for the green stems of possibility: for the intuitive hunch that may turn into a larger insight, for the glance or touch that may thaw a frozen relationship, for the stranger's act of kindness that makes the world seem hospitable again.

Spring in its fullness is not easy to write about. Late spring is so flamboyant that it caricatures itself, which is why it has long been the province of poets with more passion than skill. But perhaps those poets have a point. Perhaps we are meant to yield to this flamboyance, to understand that life is not always to be measured and meted as winter compels us to do but to be spent from time to time in a riot of color and growth.

Late spring is potlatch time in the natural world, a great giveaway of blooming beyond all necessity and reason—done, it would appear, for no reason other than the sheer joy of it.

The gift of life, which seemed to be withdrawn in winter, has been given once again, and nature, rather than hoarding it, gives it all away. There is another paradox here, known in all the wisdom traditions: if you receive a gift, you keep it alive not by clinging to it but by passing it along.

Of course, the realists will tell us that nature's profligacy always has some practical function, and that may well be so. But ever since I read Annie Dillard on the immoderation of trees, I have had to wonder. She begins with a mental exercise to help us understand how superfluous in design an ordinary tree can be—if you doubt it, she suggests, try to make a faithful scale model of the next tree you see. Then, taunting the realists, she writes: "You are God. You want to make a forest, something to hold the soil, lock up solar energy, and give off oxygen. Wouldn't it be simpler just to rough in a slab of chemicals, a green acre of goo?"[3]

From autumn's profligate seedings to the great spring giveaway, nature teaches a steady lesson: if we want to save our lives, we cannot cling to them but must spend them with abandon. When we are obsessed with bottom lines and productivity, with efficiency of time and motion, with the rational relation of means and ends, with projecting reasonable goals and making a beeline toward them, it seems unlikely that our work will ever bear full fruit, unlikely that we will ever know the fullness of spring in our lives.

And when did we start to misuse that beeline metaphor? Just watch the bees work in the spring. They flit all over the place, flirting with both the flowers and their fates. Obviously, the bees are practical and productive, but no science can persuade me that they are not pleasuring themselves as well.

SUMMER

Where I live, summer's keynote is abundance. The forests fill with undergrowth, the trees with fruit, the meadows with wild flowers and grasses, the fields with wheat and corn, the gardens with zucchini, and the yards with weeds. In contrast to the sensationalism of spring, summer is a steady state of plenty, a green and amber muchness that feeds us on more levels than we know.

Nature does not always produce abundance, of course. There are summers when flood or drought destroy the crops and threaten the lives and livelihood of those who work the fields. But nature normally takes us through a reliable cycle of scarcity and abundance in which times of deprivation foreshadow an eventual return to the bountiful fields.

This fact of nature is in sharp contrast to human nature, which seems to regard perpetual scarcity as the law of life. Daily I am astonished at how readily I believe that something I need is in short supply. If I hoard possessions, it is because I believe that there are not enough to go around. If I struggle with others over power, it is because I believe that power is limited. If I become jealous in relationships, it is because I believe that when you get too much love, I will be short-changed.

Even in writing this essay, I have had to struggle with the scarcity assumption. It is easy to stare at the blank page and despair of ever having another idea, another image, another illustration. It is easy to look back at what one has written and say, "That's not very good, but I'd better keep it, because nothing better will come along." It is difficult to trust that the pool of possibilities is bottomless, that one can keep diving in and finding more.

The irony, often tragic, is that by embracing the scarcity assumption, we create the very scarcities we fear. If I hoard material goods, others will have too little and I will never have enough. If I fight my way up the ladder of power, others will be defeated and I will never feel secure. If I get jealous of someone I love, I am likely to drive that person away. If I cling to the words I have written as if they were the last of their kind, the pool of new possibilities will surely go dry. We create scarcity by fearfully accepting it as law and by competing with others for resources as if we were stranded in the Sahara at the last oasis.

In the human world, abundance does not happen automatically. It is created when we have the sense to choose community, to come together to celebrate and share our common store. Whether the scarce resource is money or love or power or words, the true law of life is that we generate more of whatever seems scarce by trusting its supply and passing it around. Authentic abundance does not lie in secured stockpiles of food or cash or influence or affection but in belonging to a community where we can give those goods to others who need them—and receive them from others when we are in need.

I sometimes speak on college campuses about the importance of community in academic life, one of the most competitive cultures I know. On one such occasion, following my talk, a man stood in the audience, introduced himself as occupant of the "Distinguished Such-and-Such Chair of Biology," and began what I thought—given his rather pompous self-introduction—would surely be an attack. Instead, he said simply, "Of course we must learn to live in community with each other. After all, it is only good biology." Biology, the discipline that was once driven by anxious metaphors like "survival of the fittest" and "nature red in tooth and claw," now has a new metaphor—community. Death has not ceased, of course, but now it is understood as a legacy to the community of abundant life.

Here is a summertime truth: abundance is a communal act, the joint creation of an incredibly complex ecology in which each part functions on behalf of the whole and, in return, is sustained by the whole. Community doesn't just create abundance—community *is* abundance. If we could learn that equation from the world of nature, the human world might be transformed.

Summer is the season when all the promissory notes of autumn and winter and spring come due, and each year the debts are repaid with compound interest. In summer, it is hard to remember that we had ever doubted the natural process, had ever ceded death the last word, had ever lost faith in the powers of new life. Summer is a reminder that our faith is not nearly as strong as the things we profess to have faith in — a reminder that for this single season, at least, we might cease our anxious machinations and give ourselves to the abiding and abundant grace of our common life.

NOTES

Gratitudes

1. Parker J. Palmer, *Seeking Vocation in Darkness and Light* (Swannanoa, N.C.: Warren Wilson College, 1999).

2. Parker J. Palmer, "On Minding Your Call—When No One Is Calling," *Weavings*, May-June 1996, pp. 15–22.

3. Parker J. Palmer, "All the Way Down: Depression and the Spiritual Journey," *Weavings*, Sept.-Oct. 1998, pp. 31–41.

4. Parker J. Palmer, *Leading from Within: Reflections on Spirituality and Leadership* (Indianapolis: Indiana Office of Campus Ministry, 1990).

5. Parker J. Palmer, *Seasons* (Kalamazoo, Mich.: Fetzer Institute, n.d.).

Chapter I

1. William Stafford, "Ask Me," from *The Way It Is: New & Selected Poems* (St. Paul, Minn.: Graywolf Press, 1998), p. 56.

2. Mohandas K. Gandhi, *An Autobiography, or the Story of My Experiments with Truth* (Ahmedabad, India: Navajivan Press, 1927).

Chapter II

1. May Sarton, "Now I Become Myself," in *Collected Poems, 1930–1973* (New York: Norton, 1974), p. 156.

2. Martin Buber, *Tales of the Hasidim: The Early Masters* (New York: Schocken Books, 1975), p. 251.

3. Frederick Buechner, *Wishful Thinking: A Seeker's ABC* (San Francisco: HarperSanFrancisco, 1993), p. 119.

4. Phil Cosineau, *The Art of Pilgrimage* (Berkeley: Conari Press, 1998), p. xxiii.

5. Parker J. Palmer, *The Company of Strangers: Christians and the Renewal of America's Public Life* (New York: Crossroads, 1981).

6. See Howard H. Brinton, *The Pendle Hill Idea: A Quaker Experiment in Work, Worship, Study* (Wallingford, Pa.: Pendle Hill, 1950), and Eleanor Price Mather, *Pendle Hill: A Quaker Experiment in Education and Community* (Wallingford, Pa.: Pendle Hill, 1980).

7. Rumi, "Forget Your Life," in *The Enlightened Heart*, ed. Stephen Mitchell (New York: HarperCollins, 1989), p. 56.

8. Rosa Parks, *Rosa Parks: My Story* (New York: Dial Books, 1992), p. 116.

Chapter III

1. For details on the conduct of a clearness committee, see Rachel Livsey and Parker J. Palmer, *The Courage to Teach: A Guide for Reflection and Renewal* (San Francisco: Jossey-Bass, 1999), pp. 43–48.

2. May Sarton, "Now I Become Myself," in *Collected Poems, 1930–1973* (New York: Norton, 1974), p. 156.

3. Quoted in Elizabeth Watson, *This I Know Experimentally* (Philadelphia: Friends General Conference, 1977), p. 16.

Chapter IV

1. Robert Pinsky, *Canto I* from *The Inferno of Dante: A New Verse Translation* (New York: Noonday Press, 1994), canto 1:1–7.

2. See, for example, Henri J. M. Nouwen, *The Inner Voice of Love: A Journey Through Anguish to Freedom* (New York: Doubleday, 1996).

3. See, for example, John 13.

4. Rainer Maria Rilke, *Letters to a Young Poet*, trans. M. D. Herter Norton (New York: W. W. Norton & Company, 1993), p. 59.

5. Florida Scott Maxwell, *The Measure of My Days* (New York: Penguin Books, 1983), p. 42.

Chapter V

1. Václav Havel, speech delivered to joint meeting of the U.S. Congress. From *The Art of the Impossible* by Václav Havel; trans. Paul Wilson et al. (New York: Alfred A. Knopf, Inc., 1997), pp. 17–18.

2. Annie Dillard, *Teaching a Stone to Talk* (New York: Harper-Collins, 1982), pp. 94–95.

3. Vincent Kavaloski and Jane Kavaloski, "Moral Power and the Czech Revolution," *Fellowship*, Jan.-Feb. 1992, p. 9.

4. See Livsey and Palmer, *The Courage to Teach: A Guide for Reflection and Renewal*, pp. 43–48.

Chapter VI

1. Rainer Maria Rilke, *Letters to a Young Poet*, trans. M. D. Herter Norton (New York: Norton, 1993), p. 35.

2. Thomas Merton, "Hagia Sophia," in *A Thomas Merton Reader*, ed. Thomas P. McDonnell (New York: Doubleday, 1989), p. 506.

3. Annie Dillard, *Pilgrim at Tinker Creek* (New York: Harper's Magazine Press, 1974), pp. 129–130.

Parker J. Palmer is a writer, teacher, and activist who works independently on issues in education, community, leadership, spirituality, and social change. His work spans a wide range of institutions—colleges and universities, public schools, community organizations, religious institutions, corporations, and foundations. He serves as senior associate of the American Association of Higher Education and senior adviser to the Fetzer Institute and is the founder of Fetzer's Teacher Formation Program for K–12 teachers.

Palmer travels widely domestically and abroad—conducting workshops, delivering lectures, leading retreats—and has often been cited as a master teacher. His work has been featured by the *New York Times*, the *Chronicle of Higher Education, Change* magazine, *Christian Century*, CBS-TV news, and the Voice of America. The Danforth Foundation, the Lilly Endowment, and the Fetzer Institute have supported his work with major grants. In 1993, he won the national award of the Council of Independent Colleges for Outstanding Contributions to Higher Education. In 1998, "The Leadership Project," a national survey of ten thousand administrators and faculty, named Palmer one of the nation's "most influential senior leaders" in higher education and one of the ten key "agenda-setters" of the past decade, declaring: "He has inspired a generation of teachers and reformers with evocative visions of community, knowing, and spiritual wholeness."

His writing has been recognized with five honorary doctorates, two Distinguished Achievement Awards from the National Educational Press Association, an Award of Excellence from the Associated Church Press, Critic's Choice citations from *Commonweal* and *Christian Century* magazines, selection by several book clubs, and translation into several languages. His publications include ten poems, more than one hundred essays, and several widely used books, including *The Promise of Paradox, The Company of Strangers, To Know As We Are Known, The Active Life,* and *The Courage to Teach.*

Palmer received his B.A. degree in philosophy and sociology from Carleton College, where he was elected to Phi Beta Kappa and was awarded a Danforth Graduate Fellowship. After a year at Union Theological Seminary, he studied sociology at the University of California at Berkeley, where he received his M.A. and Ph.D. degrees with honors. He is a member of the Religious Society of Friends (Quaker) and lives in Madison, Wisconsin.

CREDITS

A Hidden Wholeness:
The Journey Toward an Undivided Life

Parker J. Palmer

Hardcover

ISBN: 0-7879-7100-6

A BookSense Pick, September 2004

This book is a treasure—an inspiring, useful blueprint for building safe places where people can commit to "act in every situation in ways that honor the soul."—*Publishers Weekly*

"The soul is generous: it takes in the needs of the world. The soul is wise: it suffers without shutting down. The soul is hopeful: it engages the world in ways that keep opening our hearts. The soul is creative: it finds a path between realities that might defeat us and fantasies that are mere escapes. All we need to do is to bring down the wall that separates us from our own soul and deprives the world of the soul's regenerative powers."—From *A Hidden Wholeness*

At a time when many of us seek ways of working and living that are more resonant with our souls, *A Hidden Wholeness* offers insight into our condition and guidance for finding what we seek within ourselves and with each other.

PARKER J. PALMER is a highly respected writer, lecturer, teacher, and activist. His work speaks deeply to people from many walks of life, including public schools, college and universities, religious institutions, corporations, foundations, and grass-roots organizations. The Leadership Project, a 1998 survey of 10,000 American educators, named him one of the thirty most influential senior leaders in higher education and one of ten key "agenda-setters" of the past decade. Author of six previous books-including the bestsellers *Let Your Life Speak* and *The Courage to Teach*-his writing has been recognized with eight honorary doctorates and several national awards. He holds a Ph.D. from the University of California at Berkley and lives in Madison, Wisconsin.